*Always Good With a Needle:
My Journey from Radom to Redemption*

Always Good With a Needle: My Journey from Radom to Redemption

Marlene Freidenreich Kempner

As Told to Deborah Fineblum

"In the camp, I was given some raw felt and told I had to make a hat with it. I knew I better make it or else. I was scared because I had no equipment to work with. But I said to myself, 'Malka, you have to do it.' … And I did."

Always Good with a Needle: My Journey from Radom to Redemption
By Marlene Freidenreich Kempner
As Told to Deborah Fineblum

Copyright © 2015 Marlene Freidenreich Kempner
All rights reserved

**For more about Marlene Freidenreich Kempner and her story, contact
irvkempner@gmail.com.**

ISBN: 1512378232
ISBN 13: 9781512378238

Table of Contents

Introduction

I have had many names in my life. I was Marilla growing up in Poland, and Mom and my sisters called me Marilka. I liked what the teachers called me, Manya. In America I've been Marilyn, Marlene and now Marlena. Of all my names the one I like best is the one that G-d called me: Malka.

But when the conversation was in Yiddish, then I was Malkala, which is what my father always called me from the time I was small. I remember when I was packing my suitcase to leave our home in the ghetto with a boy who wanted to marry me and take me over the Russian border, my dad said, "Malkala, *gur nisht*, don't go. If you go I will not be able to live without you." As soon as he said that I unpacked my suitcase and put it away.

If you went to Radom where I was born like Irv has done you would see a Ghetto memorial to the Jews at the place where the synagogue was before the Nazis burned it down.

The shops we once owned and the homes where we once lived are still there but the Jews are not. Some of the Jewish gravestones that the Nazis had used to pave roads, Irv tells me have been returned to the Jewish cemetery. He also says there are new festivals of Jewish culture they have there but there are no Jews who come from there left to go to them. They're mostly for children of the goyim we grew up with. Except for those markers and a few Yiddish signs where Jewish hotels and restaurants once stood, he tells me there is almost nothing left in Radom to see that we were such a big part of when I was a girl. It's like it all just disappeared.

In the 40,000 Jews from Radom who were murdered by the Nazis were most of my family – my mother and my father, my brother and his wife and my oldest sister and her husband and little girl. Only my sister Frances and I lived through it all.

But now I am 91 and I have children and grandchildren and great-grandchildren. There is still the hope that I got from my father. He always taught me: "Never give up."

One

My Radom Childhood

Before the war, we had a good life.

In German, my family name Freidenreich means 'happy and rich.' And once we were. Not that we were really rich, but happy? I would say yes. I know that my people had a good name, a good reputation in Radom.

I'm the youngest of the four children in my family. My sister, Regina, was 10 when I was born on August 28, 1922, my brother David was 8 and my sister Frances was 6. I was named after Malka, my great-aunt, my father's mother's sister who died young.

Malka Handelsman was also the name of my cousin – both of us were named after the same Malka, her grandmother and my great-aunt. She was the sister of Yaakov, or Jankiel as we called him, Handelsman, my cousin who is now famous as one of the four *sonderkommandos* who made a daring plan and were able to blow up one of the crematoria in Auschwitz. They thought that destroying the crematorium would slow down the killing and for a while it did. When they were caught, they were killed but first they tortured Jankiel.

We were more religious than most of the other people in the neighborhood. Girls didn't go to synagogue then, only on holidays. I'm a bat Kohen because my dad Yitzhak HaKohen Freidenreich was a Kohen. He was a *chassid* of the Koznitzer Rabbi and, as a Kohen, he was the one who redeemed all the baby boys in our neighborhood at their *pidyon habens,*

1

when they were a month old. The Lublina Yeshiva was run by the rabbi's brother, Aaron. We were a *kavod* family, a holy family, and to be Yitzhak Freidenreich's daughter was really something! When my father's rabbi would come to Radom my parents would entertain the whole entourage. The *kinadale* (matzah balls) that my mom made for the rabbi were delicious and she could make it look so effortless. We weren't rich but anytime the rabbi would come to town, he would come to our house and eat there and bless us. I remember when Dad went to the rabbi for the last time, he blessed my dad that he "should be spared from goyishe hands and people's mouths. People talk," he told him.

Dad came from eight children: five boys and three girls. Dad was the oldest and they all respected him. On his side my great-grandfather was Chaim Moshe Korman who was an important man and successful in the leather trade and my grandfather was Elizar Freidenreich ha Kohen. My grandmother Hadassah was actually born in Radom, then Dad's whole family moved to Warsaw except for my Handelsman cousins and we were so close with them, often having *yontif* together and feeling like brothers and sisters, not cousins.

Everyone else returned to Warsaw in the mid-30s and my grandmother Hadassah died two years later so she did not live to see the war or any of the things that happened to us. It was after her that my only niece was named. Baby Hadassah was killed when she was 4 in the gas chambers at Auschwitz with her mother, my older sister Regina.

My mom was Tirtza (Mokobodzka) and she was born in the 1880s. My mother's family was from Jeziory, a village not far from Warsaw. They lived in a big house there; they were well-to-do. She was the seventh of 10: eight girls and two boys who were the youngest children. My sister Regina had known our grandparents but I didn't. But I always liked to hear stories about them. My grandfather Moshe Mokobodzka had been in the forestry business and he died about when I was born. A cousin Chaya Vita was named after my grandmother Fetah Mylech. Later they moved to Warsaw where they were wealthy selling iron used for building. They made great *shidduchim*, great marriage matches.

I remember when I was a child my mother came back from her parents' funeral with a heavy crystal wine goblet. I remember also that my mother gave up her inheritance because her sister did so poorly financially. To Chava and her 10 beautiful children my mother gave her portion of the inheritance. I also remember the wine goblet broke and I couldn't forgive myself. There were some surviving children on that side of the family but not many.

As a child I was loved so much by both my parents and maybe because I was the youngest. I also look like both my mother and father. My oldest sister Regina, she was really something. She would make a statement that my parents spoiled me, that even if I wanted to convert they would say "fine!" Mom didn't mind when we spoke Polish but my father preferred we speak in Yiddish; he was more religious. Regina spoke Polish beautifully. She had beautiful teeth and she had guts. I was afraid to talk and I would blush, but I wanted so much to be like her.

I remember that my parents wanted us to have a good life, not to have to work too hard. We lived at 61 Zeromskiego my whole childhood until the time we had to move to the ghetto with the other Jewish families in our city. But where I grew up was in a big beautiful apartment in the center of town. We had a store in front of the apartment where my parents sold leather goods – like most of my family in Warsaw, Dad was in the leather business but also sold all kinds of general merchandise including chocolates. I remember when I was 15, the wedding of Regina to David Lester. It was 1937 and Hadassah was born three years later.

I was not going to Jewish schools and I went to school and played with non-Jewish children. I wore the white blouse and navy skirt with pleats that was the school uniform. Where I went to school we went six days a week, including Saturdays. My father was the only religious man on our street and, at first my Dad did not permit me to go to school on Saturdays. But later he said, "Malka, you can go to school on Shabbos but just don't write. Sit there and listen." Even now I don't write on Shabbos because I promised my dad I wouldn't.

We had a neighbor in our building named Mrs. Goldfeder who had a daughter two years ahead of me in school who I used to play with. She was also Regina, and very good at arts and crafts and singing but this Regina did not have a tush to sit and study. There were no other Jewish kids in my school and I didn't know many but my sister, Francis, had her Bais Yaakov friends who I remember were all nice girls.

One day our neighbor Mrs. Goldfeder asked me, "Did you know you had a beautiful sister? Smart too. I used to bring down chicken soup for

Channala." Then she told me my mother had typhoid and couldn't go to Channa's funeral.

That's how I found out that I had a sister named Channa who died when she was 4, a week before I was born. When I asked my mom about Channa she said, "Children should not know about bad things."

My grandfather, my father's father, died before the war in 1929 when I was 7. He was sitting in a sukkah near his home in Warsaw when the bench broke and he fell and broke a hip. They took him to the hospital and that's where he got pneumonia and he died there.

When it was time for my brother to go in the army he starved himself, only drinking black coffee, so he would be underweight for his height and not have to go in. He did that for three years and I couldn't take it watching him starve himself.

Most of my father's family lived in Warsaw and my mother's parents lived in Radom until the 1930s which was 60 miles south of Warsaw. It was a city much smaller than Warsaw and it was a beautiful city. Even though it was very Jewish, we did not live in the Jewish neighborhoods but on one of the busiest streets, in the center of the main business area. There were about 40,000 Jews in Radom when I was growing up there. They worked in leather like my dad but also in other businesses and in professions like accounting, law, medicine and teaching, and even in the banks. The Jews had our own hospital, orphanage and old-age home and also synagogues, a cemetery, theater, libraries and religious schools plus newspapers that my father read in Yiddish.

We had Hassidim and lots of non-religious Jews in our town too. A lot of what happened to us you can read in *The Book of Radom: The Story of a Jewish Community in Poland Destroyed by the Nazis.* The man who wrote it in 1963 was Alfred Lipson, who was my cousin. I recognize so many of the people in the book, including some other cousins, neighbors from our street, friends of my sisters, the photographer who is the one who took the picture of me as a girl that hangs over my bed now and a class photo from the Jewish high school Frances had been in. Nearly every one of the children in that picture were killed in the war. My cousin's book says three-quarters of the Jews of Radom did not survive the war. I think maybe it was more.

When I was growing up, the goyim in my building they liked my parents. One of them, Irene Durashevitzh, wore medals from World War I and she would visit us, and come to us even for Shabbos. She was crazy for my brother David and would always bring my brother orders for our store. My brother used to decorate the chocolates my father sold in the store. He made them

My son Irv visiting my childhood home and my father's store in Radom

so beautiful. I still like chocolate. The entrance to the store was from the street, and there was a divider and we lived in the back in our apartment. Until the war.

My father's whole family was in the leather business. My dad's younger brother Aaron was very wealthy in Warsaw from the leather business. His wife Masha came from the Malavski family of famous singers. The brothers were known as the Malavskis. From my dad's sister, Rivka, no one of that family survived the war. Maybe in the Malavskis somebody survived.

Dad did a lot of business in Warsaw – he did wholesale trading of leather and would bring back from Warsaw the soft leathers for the shoes, leathers in different colors. People would go into the stores and order the style and the leather they wanted. He used to take a train home that would come in late at night. But, when the anti-Semitism got so bad, since he always wore a Jewish hat and a beard, we were scared for him because some of the Poles used to wait for the Jews to get off the train and beat them. So sometimes he stayed in the store then and didn't do his business in Warsaw because we were worried about what could happen to him when he would travel. I remember he did still travel after the Germans came but not as often.

You could say that, growing up, we were closest to my dad's family. He was the oldest brother, then came Esther, Aaron and Betsalel and Joshua the youngest who was so beautiful. When Joshua came to Radom one time I remember he had his coat slung over his shoulder. He was married and had a 5-year-old son when the war started. I don't know what happened to them but I can guess.

I remember just after I turned 7 we were in Warsaw for the high holidays. I remember I wore a wide brimmed hat (dashik), black with red lining. It was 1929, the last time I saw my grandfather alive, just before just he fell and died of pneumonia. Before that we had a few weeks vacationing at my aunt's summer place in Otvosk, a famous place near Warsaw and my grandfather said to me in Yiddish, "Malkala, as long as you are in Warsaw, don't wear that goyish hat."

My older sister Regina was married to David Lesser and his younger sister Paula was Regina's sister-in-law and they were very close. When my sister and David got engaged, there was a store available and he and his brother Pincus opened the big book store United there. It was down the street from us across from the courthouse on Zeromskiego Street. David and his older brother Pincus ran that store and their sister Paula took over the small book store they used to run. The brother's wife was also Regina so both brothers were married to Reginas, they also both had the Jewish name of Rivka. Both couples were married in 1937. Regina and her David had baby Hadassah in December of 1940.

The older brother of the other Regina who was Regina Winder Lesser, often came to our house before the war. His name was Marek Winder. He decided to go to Palestine and left shortly before the war in 1939. The Winders were wealthy people and, after the war began, he once offered to pay for my brother David's expenses to go to Palestine. He would have gone but my oldest sister was married and if my brother would gone he would have left me alone with my parents and Frances. So he wouldn't leave us. Marek Winder came back to Poland after the war and many years later I stayed in his house in Israel with Tes when she was 12.

I was always very close with Frances. I understood she was sick when she was born, and I always felt like I was stronger than her and needed to take care of her, even though she was older. My parents took her all kinds of doctors and she got well and stayed well until the war. As a matter of fact she was the only one of us sisters who was very religious; she was a secretary at Bais Yaakov. I remember she was very religious and had fine religious friends.

I was in Warsaw the summer of 1939 just before the war broke out. We would have gone back for the High Holidays in September if the war had not started then. I had just turned 17 that August.

Two

The Nazis Take Radom: September 8, 1939

I remember when the Nazis took over Radom. It was a Friday morning a week after my 17th birthday and we were getting ready for Shabbos. All of a sudden the Polish soldiers were gone and the Germans were there. We could see their tanks rolling down our street.

We didn't realize that day what it would mean to us and our lives. But, even though we didn't live in a Jewish neighborhood, we heard that, even the first days they were there, the Germans were already dragging Jews into the street and forcing them to do this or that job, most of them just made up to humiliate them. Or they would cut off their beards and push them down, especially the older men. And then we heard that we Jewish kids weren't allowed to go to school anymore and we saw the flag with the swastika up in the town. Many of the Poles, even some of them I had grown up with in the neighborhood, began to side with the Nazis and also do these things.

We also heard about other things that the Nazis were doing: beating up men if they removed their hat and beating them up if they didn't. That year, we could not hold services for Rosh Hashana and Yom Kippur and the shuls were emptied of Torahs and the Nazis used them for stables and store rooms for their horses. You could imagine what that did to my dad. When Jews did come together to pray in someone's home, the Nazis dragged the men out by their talises and beat them up. We heard that they tried to force some Jews to eat pork and, if they refused, they were beaten and then shot.

8

All Jews needed to be registered and they set up offices and a Judenrat, a council of Jews to carry out their orders. The Jewish community had to pay huge taxes and give the Germans their bedding and anything else their soldiers needed.

It only took a few weeks for more new laws to come down to us. Jews were not allowed to own a radio, and we had to wear armbands with Jewish stars on our coats and we could be killed if we refused to wear them. (I did go without one once, when my parents sent me on a dangerous trip to Warsaw because they were hearing such terrible things about what was happening with our family there. I will tell you about that later.) Also there could be no more kosher butchering of meat, and Jews could not walk on the sidewalks, only in the street. And, besides not being allowed to go to the public schools, all the Jewish schools, like the one Frances had gone to, were closed down. Plus we were not allowed to travel unless we got a special permit. Also we weren't allowed to walk even in the street of the main streets, and remember we *lived* on one of the main streets. Many of the younger, stronger adults were taken for laborers which the Judenrat had to arrange. Food was rationed and, because we were Jews, we got much fewer rations than our Polish neighbors.

They also closed our hospital and we could not go to the doctor's anymore. That first winter it was bitter cold and we heard that many of the Jews of Radom tried to escape to the Soviet Union, but many of them were killed or taken into forced labor there. Some of them came back to Radom because what was happening to the Jews in the Soviet Union sometimes turned out to be just as bad, or maybe even worse than in Radom.

Every night I could hear my parents whispering and I could tell they were upset and frightened. They tried so hard to protect us, to shelter us, especially me as the youngest child, but could only do only so much. Our lives were just changing too fast to not notice even if I was only 17. And since she was 10 years older than me, Regina knew a lot more about what was going on and David too, being eight years older. Sometimes they told Frances and me things I don't think my parents wanted us to know.

Warsaw

Things were very bad in Warsaw even before they got bad in Radom. Around the end of December of 1939, just a couple of months after the

Nazis came, a friend of my parents from Warsaw wrote to us about the deaths of one of my uncles and my grandmother and there were other letters from the family that really worried my parents. Also people came back from there saying terrible things. So my parents let me go see what was happening with our family there. What I did was very dangerous: I traveled without my armband to Warsaw – and my parents agreed to it – because we had to know what was happening there.

When I got there I found my Uncle Aaron's home bombarded. My uncle had been a successful leather trader and his home had been a very nice one before the war. When I got there he told me about the bombing and how he'd recognized his wife's hands in the rubble near the house after a bomb hit and how he got help pulling her out. She went to live with her wealthy relatives, the Kotlivskys to recuperate. When I was in his house, Uncle Aaron had heard a rumor the Nazis were there in the neighborhood searching for Jews. Uncle Aaron hid me and my cousin in the dust-and-ash drawer of the oven so when the Nazis came they didn't find anyone. I remember that my aunt Moravsky gave me $100 to buy my ticket home to Radom and told me to give the rest to her family, the Cantors. I also managed to travel home without an armband. As dangerous as it was, if you were a Jew it was the only way you could travel outside your own ghetto. My cousin, Uncle Betsalel's daughter Helena or Helinka (I think her Jewish name was Channah) was 10 and so smart. When things were already so bad in Warsaw my uncle sent her by herself to us and she stayed a while. I carried the whole responsibility of her while she was there and I was scared. Then she went back to Warsaw and I never heard anything about what happened to her.

My uncle Aaron wrote a letter in Yiddish to my father that he wanted him to find the wife of a certain man without legs in the hospital. I was able to find her and bring her back to Radom to see her husband. I had such *rachmonos* that I was able to bring her. The train came to a stop at Demblim. They were looking for people. I kept saying I am not Jewish. My Uncle Aaron's letter I hid.

My mother's older sister Chava Moshevitz and her religious son Motel – he was probably just a little older than bar mitzvah – were killed in the street in Warsaw early on with all the bombing that was happening there. They were found on the street by her 5-year-old grandson who stood over her yelling, "Grandmother, get up! Grandmother get up!" We learned this from a family friend from Warsaw who sent us a letter saying they had died. Out of my dad's whole big family only a few of my cousins survived.

Things kept getting worse and worse for both sides of our Warsaw family. My father's little brother Joshua died of shrapnel that came in through the window when he was sleeping. It killed him instantly. Joshua's 5-year-old old son, my cousin, was taken to the Warsaw ghetto where we think he either died of starvation or was murdered in Treblinka during one of the actions. My grandmother, my father's mother, died of a heart attack, of a broken heart really, just eight days after her son Joshua was killed. My teenaged cousin Yaakov had gone in search of his mother when he was hit in the leg with shrapnel, and his leg had to be amputated. Later he walked with a limp and a prosthesis.

Once Dad's sister Elka came to visit. She had a 5-year-old child. Dad had sent her money to make herself a suit and she came to Radom wearing that blue suit. My dad would do anything for family.

But, as terrible as things were in Warsaw, even in Radom by then there were so many beatings and people being shot in the street for no reason. My mother was afraid my father's beard would get him beaten, and begged him to let her cut it. But he wouldn't hear of it.

Since Jews were not allowed to own stores anymore, especially on main streets, my brother-in-law David and his brother asked my sister's non-Jewish friends who ran a movie house if they could put a non-Jew in to run the brothers' big shop, United Bookstore.

Of course, ours was not a Jewish neighborhood and my dad was the most religious person on the block. The owners of the apartment house were real anti-Semites and their oldest son made all the Jews leave. But we kept paying our rent directly to his younger brother who was friendly with us and so we were able to stay until April of 1941 when all the Jews were sent to the ghetto. During this year-and-a-half, since Jewish children were not allowed to go to school anymore, I tried to teach myself. I asked my goyish friends what they were learning and tried to learn it too, taking notes from what they said.

The Jews had to give up our jewelry during this time but my father took the jewelry he had and a few coins and had them melted down into rings for Frances and me that had each of our initials: MF and FF. I would lose my ring in the camps when a man who wanted me to go away with him got mad and ripped it off my finger. I will tell you more about how that happened soon. I found Frances' ring in her house after she died. I have no idea, after everything we went through, how she was able to save it from being taken.

All this time I was sort of angry with the goyim I was raised with, since most of my friends growing up were goyim. Starting when the Germans came, many of my friends in the neighborhood began turning away when they'd see me in the street. In Polish they'd say, "*Ona jeszcze?* – she's still here?" That's how they greeted us. Even in our neighborhood, we knew that so many Jews were being killed and how many of the goyim, along with the Germans, the Polish police and civilians too were taking their property.

What I did not know was that this was going to be the last time I would ever live in the home I grew up in. And, by the time we had to go to the ghetto, things were just getting worse and worse for us and all the Jews in Radom.

Three

We Are Forced into the Ghetto: April, 1941

I was always good with a needle, and so were both my sisters, which saved us so many times. Of course, it's not what our parents wanted for us. Not at all. They didn't want us to have to work hard. They wanted us to have a good life. But still it saved us many, many times. Frances and I were lucky. We lived through the whole war. David and his wife were taken in the first liquidation on August, 5, 1942, my parents 12 days later, in the second liquidation. And Regina and her little girl when we got to Auschwitz. Only Frances and I lived through it all.

But in 1941 we didn't know any of this would happen. There had been rumors that all the Jews in the city were going to be moved to the other side of Radom, away from our street, and into one of the Jewish neighborhoods. When there was one week to go before Pesach (April 3), we had to move into Peretza Street 14. All I remember of that day was that I was in our old apartment alone (I guess I was 18 then) and was so happy when I saw Frances coming to get me and take me to our new place in the ghetto. We didn't know then that we would live there for a year and a half, until the ghetto was liquidated – the second liquidation when they came for my parents.

Our place was on a street in the larger of the two Jewish ghettos in Radom. My brother had connections and always had a lot of friends wherever he went, including the man who was now president of the ghetto. So

13

because of him they gave us a good place. We had two rooms for the four of us (my parents, Frances and me) and one of them was our own kitchen which many people didn't have. There was also room for a small shop in the front facing the street, a separate store entrance and also a window and counter for customers. In that store my father sold rations like sugar and flour and also tobacco and a few other things. Because of my brother's connections, my dad got distribution rights to sell those rations from this little shop.

The owners of the building, the Kadishevitz family, were Jewish and they had four children, one of them a little girl who could not walk. She stayed all day in their house in a special chair.

I remember there was a divider with a red curtain between the kitchen and our other room. My parents put it up between the stove and cabinet and the white credenza and the beds to make it like a second room. I slept on the couch and Frances slept in the bed with my mother. My father was in the other bed. It wasn't much but as I said, it was better than most people had. There was a whole set of holy books on a small shelf since my father was a Kohen and very learned and religious and needed his books. He had two sets of tefillin which he put on one after the other every morning before he ate breakfast. Even in the ghetto my dad was the one called upon to redeem the month-old baby boys (in a *pidyon ha ben* ceremony) and no matter what he always returned the fee to the fathers.

For Pesach my dad made the wine out of raisins, soaking them for days in a big glass jar. He set up a linen pouch with a funnel and the raisin water dripped through it bit by bit. I can still see it dripping in the corner of the room. It was the most delicious wine I ever tasted.

Frances and I helped make Passover happen that year too. It was such a heartache that we couldn't make a real Pesach and Dad especially was upset. We had left behind our Pesach dishes in the basement of our old apartment and my sister Frances and I decided to do something very dangerous: we left the ghetto without our armbands. We wouldn't go to the main street which was patrolled but went around a narrow alleyway to the back of our old apartment. With our hands we enlarged a small hole in the barbed wire. I got cut on the barbed wire and still have the scar. I was bleeding but we kept going. We climbed in the basement window and whatever we could carry of our Pesach dishes we took. We would never let our goyish neighbors know we were there. They had been our friends but we had stopped trusting them. I remember we tried to make ourselves invisible that night, carrying all those dishes back to the ghetto.

Somehow my dad got some matzos and we also somehow got meat and gefilte fish, and with the raisin wine he made it was delicious. It's a miracle that with everything that was happening, still we managed to have a real Pesach that year.

The Letter

Since there was no school for me, I was always knitting and crocheting with wool yarn to make sweaters and other things to keep us warm, and doing embroidery. I was knitting something one day when there was a knock on the door. A man who was very well dressed for the circumstances stood there saying he was David Kempner and he'd been told there was a letter for him that had been delivered to us. And that my mom who was working in the store had told him to come around the back and knock and her daughter would know where the letter was. I found it and gave it to him and he was really nice, a real gentleman which is mostly what I remember of that first time we met. All these years later I'm not sure who the letter was from, though I think it was probably from my cousin Nuta who'd

known Mr. Kempner in Warsaw. Maybe the letter was a way of introducing him to us or it may have been about some kind of business dealings with my dad's shop or maybe it was a warning from Nuta – later he told me he'd been involved in smuggling and the Germans had found out so it was no longer safe for him to show his face in Warsaw. I thought of him as a grown man when we met for the first time since I was still a teenager and he seemed so grown up. There were 12 years between us.

I never saw him again in Radom. At least I don't remember seeing him again there. Although he told me later that he'd been a few more times to my parents' store after that.

My husband David as a young man

15

The next time I remember seeing him was in Blizyn and by then I no longer had parents or a brother.

One Friday night before my brother got married we were sitting around the table with a feeling of such *kovod* (holiness). I enjoyed so much looking at my dad's face and my brother's face sitting next to him. We did not rush. Friday night, Shabbos night, for us was such a celebration, not fancy especially after we got to the ghetto, but every time we felt like such a holy people. There was a knock on the door; it was a friend of mine, a girl from a very wealthy family. She said to come out for a walk. Except on Friday night I had on my Friday night robe, mine was green, Frances' was pink. I said, "Will you wait?" It was wintertime. I got dressed and she was with a boy I didn't remember seeing before. He said he had met me in Warsaw and came to look for me. When the bombarding started there he came to make sure we were alright, he said and then he pleaded with my parents to let me go with him to Russia. He worked for an important company. So he met with my mother in Regina's apartment and my mother said ''yes'' and told me that he'll marry me and take me to Russia, and Regina also agreed. So I took out my suitcase and started putting in my clothes but part of me was not happy to leave my home and my family. My dad came over to me and said, "Malkala, please don't go. I will not be able to live without you." When he said those words, I took my clothes out of the suitcase. His sister survived but he did not and later she asked me for copies of photos of him and me to remember him by.

David's wedding

My brother David didn't get married till 1942, on February 8, when we were already in the ghetto a while. He married Liva Baum from a very fine family. I remember their wedding. It was in Liva's parents' apartment, three houses away (#67). The building belonged to a Jewish family, the Reichmans. There was no music; it was the ghetto. We walked from our place to their place and I remember Mrs. Reichman came over to my father and said about my brother, "Mr. Freidenreich, you don't know who you possess." Everyone loved my brother.

We called my brother Duvchu (a child's name) at home but he called himself Duvid, which is Yiddish. He was not religious, but my mom said,

"His goodness is better than somebody else's religion." He did so much for people. People adored him, Jews and non-Jews too. He and Liva were only married for a few months before they were taken.

Later this square became the entrance to the ghetto. Before the war Liva's family the Baums lived in the building of the Friends of Knowledge School, the Jewish school Frances went to. The two Baum boys survived, Kalman and Moshe (Monyak). I met Monyak in a camp, I think it was Wolanow. After their wedding David and Liva were given a nice apartment in the ghetto, but just for a short time and they were chased out from there. Then they moved into an apartment near us. Since my brother and older sister were married then, it was just Frances and me and my parents in our place. There was a shack and a cow in the building across the yard and my sister Frances couldn't take the smell of the cow. It got so she wouldn't even eat. But it wasn't just the cow. She could not accept what had happened to us.

Regina's dress shop was in a row of shops on the border of the large ghetto. Before we were all moved into the ghetto she had had a very nice shop at 9 Zeromskeig, a major shopping street where the rich women of the city came to have their dresses made by her. She was that good. Now the ghetto location of her shop was situated in such a way as to be accessible to German and Polish officers coming in to shop from the free areas of Radom. These were the ones who were high ranking enough to get special passes to enter the ghetto. My brother David would sometimes remove his armband and smuggle goods into the ghetto.

Then a woman from the Jewish council, the Judenrat, swore if the children would work voluntarily they would not touch the parents. I felt it was my responsibility and around Pesach of 1942 I volunteered to go to work in the Kromolowsky saddle factory.

One day at the factory I walked into the boss' office and his feet were on the desk. "I want you to know I have very capable parents," I said with tears in my eyes because I was afraid what might happen to them. "My dad understands leather very well and mom is a good cook who could help in the kitchen." I had noticed a wealthy religious woman from our town working in the factory kitchen and I asked her how she got the job. She said in Yiddish, "My *kind*, what can I tell you? One tries out the case. And one buys it with money." I didn't know what kind of money she was talking about. You had to know the right person to approach, she said. The boss said "Bring them in." I was overjoyed – the woman in the kitchen was much more old-fashioned looking and my mom looked more modern. My mom would have gone but when I told them, my dad said, "Do you expect me to eat trafe? I said, "Mom, then you come." She said, "I am not going to leave Father alone." And then she said to me, "What can I do? You go and let's hope!"

First Liquidation

But there was one day when I knew something was wrong, that something bad was going to happen. On the way home from the saddle factory that night, I saw the Germans on our side of the ghetto, in the Jewish office looking over the books, and I knew. It turned out that they were getting ready for the first liquidation of our ghetto. It was Aug. 5, 1942.

Terrified Jews during a liquidation or round-up

When I got home that night my mom was asleep and Frances was asleep and my dad was sitting on the couch, looking so peaceful. Sitting by a small petroleum light he was packing tobacco into cigarette papers using a small tube left over from World War I. I realized something was cooking, G-d knows what and I think my dad knew it too. My brother's brother-in-law who worked for a German dentist had told my brother that there was going to be an action and what they would do to the Jews.

My brother came over to pick up his good suits and warn us about what he'd heard. And when he turned to go, I begged him to stay with us but he said he had to get back to Liva. They were at number 20, and we were at 14. By this time my mother and sister were awake. None of us ever saw him again after that. My dad wanted to give some kids money to look for my brother but it never happened. Both of Liva's bothers, Kalmon and

18

Moshe (Monyk) survived but not Esther (Ethusha) who was in Auschwitz with Frances and me. We were like three sisters, not two. She was two years older than Liva and such a fine person.

After my brother left, we heard shouts and shots and suddenly I noticed that my father's beard had turned whiter overnight and his face had gotten paler. I thought that, looking the way he did, they are going to kill him right away. I knew he could not survive hard labor. He had a delicate stomach and he wasn't strong. I was scared but I remembered that we were told if the child worked the parents were safe.

I wanted to make it look like we had left the apartment in a hurry. So Frances left the narrow window open and I messed up the beds to make it look like we'd left quickly. I told my parents and Frances to hide under the table and I hid behind the mahogany room divider with the red curtain, peeking out.

From there I could hear the Nazis in the yard, then I saw them look in the window. Not seeing anyone, they left. After a night of terrible screaming and crying and the sound of shots and corpses being piled up in the streets, suddenly it was all still, such a silence like there was no one left but us. I did not know it then but that night I saved my parents for another 12 days. Until the next action. I thought then, "Did I do the right thing? Maybe there are no more Jews left. Then a cousin's son, maybe 12 years old, who worked in the ammunition factory, came running up the street to see if we were alright. He said he was glad to see us alive and told us there *were* still Jews left in Radom.

This turned out to be the first liquidation in Radom. We heard later that 10,000 Jews were sent to Treblinka that night which must have also included my brother and Liva. Others were left alive to work in forced labor camps and factories.

Remember I told you about my parents' good friend Irene Duraschevitzh who lived in our building when I was growing up? The one who was not Jewish but came to us all the time, even for Shabbos, the one who always wore the medals? She had once admired a fur coat my brother was wearing and asked him for it. But he told her that our cousin, Stanley Handelsman, had asked him to keep it for him when he was drafted into the Polish army. Then one day I ran into her just after my brother was taken. I fell into her arms crying that David was gone. And what did she say to me? "And he wouldn't give me the coat?" It's something I have never been able to forget.

The Second Liquidation

So, even though I saved them that one night, like I said it was only for 12 days. In those 12 days we saw the corpses in the street and heard more about where the rest of the Jews were sent. But of course there was no sign of my brother or Liva. Each day I didn't want to go back to work but each day my mother insisted I go and walked me to the gate where we got picked up. I remember that on the morning of the second deportation, I was so focused on saving them. But, despite all my arguments about why I should stay home that day, my mom said, "Don't worry. Just go! People would pay with gold to have your job." I know she did it because she wanted to make sure I could save myself. Working in the saddle factory saved my life that day. We were locked in the saddle factory that night, sleeping piled up on top of each other on straw in the attic.

The second liquidation was much bigger than the first. I read later that 1,500 Jews were buried in the park over three days in August and another 20,000 taken by train to be "resettled" most likely at Treblinka. I still don't know which my parents were. We also heard they took the patients from the Jewish hospital to the park and shot them, including 82-year old Judge Josef Beckerman. He was the grandson of the hospital's founder.

But I didn't know any of this then because they kept us in the saddle factory while it was going on, for maybe two weeks, and would not let us leave. One day a Jewish policeman we knew came to the factory. The Poles who used to be the friends of the Jews were worse than the Germans. Now they had the opportunity to be leaders in their black uniforms – and they did more than their duty. But this Jewish policeman everyone trusted and we all asked him to tell us if he knew anything about our families. Finally I got to speak with him face to face and he told me that my parents were taken but that he was certain my two sisters and Regina's husband and her child were still alive.

I could not accept that I would never see my parents again. I was doing knitting, making clothing for the wives and children of the officers when one day the Jewish policeman came and took me back to my sisters. I was so stiff and weak and my legs didn't carry me but I heard my sisters were alive and working in the shops on Rynek Square (Shpitalna and Jitnya Streets). Regina had gotten Frances a job there with Esthershah Baum, Liva's sister. Regina was back to making fancy tailored clothes for the officers' wives and children. Frances lived with them and she was short enough to sleep in the baby's crib with Regina and her husband and child in one bed and his brother Pincus Lesser in the other, the same brother who had run the United Book Store with him. Pincus' wife and 2-year-old son had already been taken. I slept on the floor in the kitchen though sometimes I slept in the crib and Frances slept on the kitchen floor.

I had been listed as missing from the factory so I went back but after maybe 10 days back at the factory (we were still sleeping piled on top of each other in the attic), I realized I could not live alone without my sisters and decided that whatever would be would be. I just needed to be with family. I was sick – my legs didn't hold me and I'd stopped menstruating – and I pretended to be more sick and the police brought me back to my sisters a second time. Regina had gotten her husband a job as a Jewish policeman. One day he had an order to take Jews but he couldn't do it so they fired him.

But I had no papers to work there. Several times there were searches when Frances and I hid on the Regina's roof. Then Frances got the typhoid and Regina hid her so no one would discover she was sick. Once a week there was a required bathhouse visit for anyone working on Germans' clothing, so you wouldn't infest them. But Frances was too sick to go and the Germans found her in the apartment sewing. So they beat her which caused her years of neck and back problems later on.

But since I had snuck away from my factory job and didn't go back — I needed to be with my sisters – I was illegal and couldn't be hired anywhere else. And I knew Regina couldn't employ both Frances and me anyway. But Monyk (Moshe) Novapolsky who was a good-looking, smart young man who liked me and looked out for me wrote a letter telling the Germans I did good needlework. Monyk had a good job, the Nazis let him go outside the ghetto as a messenger and he had a mother in the ghetto who he looked out for and was able to keep her alive. When he found out I was back from the saddle factory, he wrote the letter saying I was very good at crocheting and knitting and embroidery which saved me before I could be caught and sent to the gas chambers.

A German commanding officer named Rube read the letter and that's how I got to Wolanow.

Four

Wolanow and Blizyn Concentration Camps: Winter - Summer, 1943

Things were getting worse and worse for us in the ghetto. Near the end of the time we lived there, one day a policeman came and told me I was needed to make something for an officer's wife outside the ghetto and had to be taken to her for a fitting … I was working for Regina then.

After more than a year away from it, it was a strange feeling to see the building I grew up in, to see the store that used to be our store all the time I was growing up. I was taken to an apartment at No. 67, down the street from our old one and there was a woman on her hands and knees scrubbing the floor in the front hall. I recognized her immediately. She used to be a wealthy Jewish girl, my older sister Regina's friend. She recognized me too, I could tell, but she didn't say anything to me and I didn't say anything to her. The German woman who lived there just looked at me and reached out to pat my hair. "Why are you Jewish?" she said to me. She must have thought it was too bad that she had to hate me. I just looked at her. What could I answer her? She told me that she was not supposed to let me out of the ghetto but had asked as a special favor to let me come to her to do her work. Then she gave me work to do. I forget what it was that I made for her. As long as we could produce, they needed us and we were allowed to live.

You know that, after working for her, I was glad to be back in the ghetto, to be back with my people. It had been terrible being on my street that day since it brought back so many memories of being a child there, but it was no longer my street.

I must have done a good job for her since the handsome young man Monyk Novapolsky who had such a good job carrying messages in and out of the ghetto and had a mother he took care of in the ghetto wrote that letter to Rube, the commandant of Wolanow, a labor camp very close to Radom. Monyk warned us that something very bad was coming for the Jews and told me he was going to try and establish for me a place to do knitting. He pleaded with the Germans to get me out before I would be sent to the gas chambers. The letter he wrote described all the kinds of things I knew how to make. It was because of that letter that a while after my parents were taken and I moved in with Regina and her family and Frances that I was picked up and taken to Wolanow.

As soon as I got there, they put me in a room with a dress maker and a few tailors. In that room we made things for Commandant Rube's family and the families of the other high ranking officers at the camp. I was told exactly what to knit, crochet and paint for the wives and the children and even the little girls' dolls. They kept us separate from the other people in the camp, and they told us to stay away from the "dirty Jews." They wanted to keep us clean since we were working with the clothing and dolls for their families. We were given a better place to sleep, much larger than anything where I had been living in the ghetto. I still think about that German commandant Rube who every morning at roll call picked 10 people to be killed that day. He was the same man who liked to come into our room and stand there watching me knitting or embroidering. "Froilein Freidenreich, don't rush," he always said. "If it doesn't take two weeks it can take three weeks." I was knitting and crocheting clothing for his children so he wanted me to do a good job; he didn't want me to rush.

Once there was another woman named Freidenreich in the camp, a distant relative, who had run away, and one of the guards hearing my name said, "We are looking for her!" I was afraid but Commandant Rube came and said I wasn't her and showed them the clothing I was making, so they left me alone after that.

Typhoid got to be terrible in the camp after I got there and whoever was found to have it was immediately killed. Remember Novapolsky who was able to go around without an armband and travel outside the ghetto for the Nazis, the one who wrote the letter about me? After he had gotten permission for me to come and sew and knit for the officers' families, he was beaten terribly and got typhoid. He died soon afterwards but his mother who he was so worried about, she survived the war.

At the camp I saw a lot of the Poles from our town who now worked for the Nazis. The Poles who used to be the friends of the Jews before the war sometimes were worse than the Germans. Now that they had an opportunity to be leaders and bosses, they often did more than their duty to the Jews. I was friends then with Chanya from Radom – they took her in the end.

There was one guard who was always talking to me and wanted to save me, a member of the intelligentsia in charge of us. He was in love with me and he told me if I survive the war he would marry me. But when I asked a question once he said to me, "Why do you think so Jewish?" When I told him I had to turn him down since I could never marry a non-Jew, I said: "Better I should go up in smoke in the chimney." He was so angry that he grabbed my finger and pulled off the ring with MF on it that my father had had made for me. Did I tell you that I found the FF one that belonged to Frances in her things after she died? Somehow – I don't know how – she had kept it all those years.

Blizyn Uniform Factory

I was in Wolanow for about half a year, from winter to summer. Then I was sent to the Blizyn labor camp to work in their uniform factory and I was there for maybe four or five months. In Blizyn I worked on the Nazi uniforms. Luckily I was handy with a needle and it didn't take long for me to understand what was going on and how to do what they needed. They kept us in the factory until very late every night.

Pretty soon after I got there I met a young woman from Radom, Renya Veximan, who had been there a while and had a good place in the bunk. I wanted the top bunk always because people would pee in the night and if you were under them you got peed on which is a terrible feeling.

Blizyn was the next time I saw David Kempner. He was not very tall so he was usually in the front of the line at roll call. Every day when I saw him I said to myself, "I know this man." But instead of being in an elegant suit, now he was in stripes. Then I remembered where and when I'd met him, at my father's store in the ghetto when he came for his letter. Then one morning he didn't show up for work detail. But it was a very hot day, so there was no work and also no food that day. They said at 5:00 there will be a roll call. I was waiting for it to start, sitting on the ground in a big field with a knapsack and two friends. A few men were sitting a few feet away. One of them was my future husband. He came over to talk to one of the girls he had met in Radom but I didn't say anything. Then he took out his knapsack a few pictures of himself as he was before, in a beautiful fur-lined coat. And everyone began reminiscing. I took my album from my knapsack and he said, "May I?" And I said, "Please do." Then he saw a picture of my cousin Nuta, and he looks at it and looks at me and says, "How do you come to have this picture?" And I say, "That's my cousin Nuta from Warsaw." He takes another look at me and says, "Wait a minute. You are from Radom." I say, "Yes." He says, "I was at your house," and I say "I think so too."

One day at roll call they announced they needed 70 weavers to repair ammunition baskets in a factory in Radom and instantly my hand went up. In fact, when they asked who is an experienced weaver, each one of us from Radom raised our hands. We were told we needed to pass an examination to make sure we really could repair damaged ammunition baskets. A Jewish man named Guterman was a real weaver and he taught me in Polish how to repair them. After the examination, all the people who had said they were weavers but didn't how to do it were put on a bench and lashed 70 times. I saw men stripped naked put on the bench and whipped with men holding down their hands if they failed the exam. That's what happened if you failed. My friend, Renya Veximan, was one of the people who got beaten for saying she could repair them because she wanted so badly to go back to Radom. One woman said about me, "She has no idea what to do," because she wanted her sister-in-law to get my spot. I was so afraid of how I would do on the examination that I ran to the back of the line. When I was finally called I was trembling. My luck was that Mr. Guterman who really was a basket weaver had showed me how to hold the straw and how to weave it across the empty space after that. In the exam I did it the way he had taught me and afterwards the German said, "Call back Fraulein Freidenreich!" because I had passed but also maybe because he liked my name. It sounded very German.

In the end they took only 40 of us and we heard that some people had died from the lashings. People in the camp were saying it was a trick and they were just going to take us back to the barracks and kill us. But I had to take a chance that I could possibly go back to where my sisters were.

I went to find Mr. Kempner to say good-bye and he asked me not to go. He also thought it was a trap and very dangerous, and that I would be safer staying where I was. I said I had to go to my sisters and whatever would happen to them would happen to me too. Knowing he could not stop me, Mr. Kempner gave me his blessing and he said, "If we live I will find you." The next day they took us and one of the guards gave me an apple; my G-d, an apple!

After the war I was in Toronto visiting my friend Guta Lindson who married a Letterman. All of a sudden a tall elegant lady came across the street and Guta said, "Don't you know who this is? It's Renya Veximan from Radom!" I said "Renya!" She said "Marilla!" She lived in a fancy neighborhood and the next day she came to take us to her house. She knew my cousins Monya and Bracha Handelsman (I was named after their grandmother, my great-aunt Malka), who also survived and also lived in Toronto.

But for now I was back in Radom at the basket factory.

Five

BACK IN RADOM: SUMMER, 1943-WINTER, 1944

After being alone in Wolanow and Blizyn, even with my parents and brother gone, I was so glad to be back in Radom. At least I still had my sisters, my brother-in-law David and my little niece Hadassah.

But when I got there I could see how bad things were for them. Frances was still sewing for Regina but Regina had kept Frances hidden since her typhoid fever because anyone caught with typhoid was automatically taken out and shot. When the Nazis discovered Frances at home sewing on the machine, they told Regina they were going to deport Frances. Regina kissed the boots of the commandant and told him: "If you kill my sister I will not be able to work." And, since Regina was such a talented dressmaker who all the officers' wives and girlfriends relied on, they knew they had better leave Frances alone.

So, even though it was good to be together again and not feel all alone in the world, by that winter things were getting worse and worse in Radom. My brother-in-law lost his job that Regina had gotten him in the printing plant when that shop was closed. Then he had nothing and that meant we would not be allowed to stay in the ghetto any longer. That's when my sister decided to give up her shop. One day she closed it up and the five of us left Radom, traveling sometimes on foot and other times in a wagon, until we got to the prison at Szydlowicz.

27

Meanwhile while we were gone, what we didn't know was that my sister Regina's customers were coming to the shop looking for her – she had left maybe 100 dresses unfinished. Her customers, the wives and the girlfriends of the top German and Polish officers, were all complaining and one of them said, "Why did you take my Regina? You could have taken 100 other *shmutzik* (dirty) Yidden instead and left us our Regina!"

We were only there in Szydlowicz a day or two – there were so many people that we had to sleep on top of each other – when a truck arrived with orders to take Regina back to Radom along with her husband and child. But Frances and I, we were not on the list. There was a big tumult when she said, "What about Marilla and Franya, my sisters?" She went into the commandant's office and was in there a long time pleading with him to let us come too. That whole time I was holding the child wrapped in a big shawl of my mother's and she was trying hard to wiggle out of my arms. She was very smart, the baby, and was talking already. She said to me in Polish, "Aunt Marilla, I'm not afraid of Shavilsky (the German officer in charge of Regina's shop). Did you know, Aunt Marilla, that Shavilsky gave me a big chocolate bar and told me to hide it but quick!"

After a while when Regina didn't come back, Frances and I decided we had to do something. So we jumped onto the open truck as if we had a right to be there. I told Frances to lie down flat on the floor of the truck and, thinking that since I was holding the child, they wouldn't stop me, I sat there with her still covered in the shawl to try to keep her quiet and maybe go to sleep. When Regina and David finally got into the truck Regina looked heartbroken (she later told us they had told her no, we could not come with them back to Radom). I could see how surprised she was to see us in the truck but she was careful not to show it … you know the Jewish mind is sharp, especially in a crisis. She just climbed in and didn't say anything but I could tell how relieved she was to see us there.

When we got near Radom, Frances and I jumped off the truck (by this time Regina had the child) because we knew that when they stopped they were going to take roll call and, since we were not on the list, it would be the end for us and bad for Regina too. It took a long time at night to walk to Regina and David's apartment at Shpital 9 and when we got there we found her brother-in-law, David's older brother Pincus there. The next day

Regina went back to her shop to finish the dresses and make her customers happy and she was able to get David a job.

Frances as the smallest of us would sleep in the crib (the baby was in the bed with her parents and Pincus had the other bed). And I would sleep on the kitchen floor or sometimes we would take turns and I would sleep in the crib and Frances would sleep on the kitchen floor. But we were not on the list of people permitted to stay in Radom, which was only for the people who were working for the Nazis. So there were days when Frances and I hid under the beds and once when the Nazis came to inspect for escapees we ran up to the attic to hide whenever we'd hear a noise. There were a couple of other close calls too, such as when the Jewish police wouldn't let Frances and me in to the ghetto, since we were not on the permitted list. Once we able to sneak in, but Regina didn't know we were there. We did not know how long we could keep this up without being found out and getting our sister into very big trouble that maybe she would not be able to get out of this time.

One time I met a friend of my brother-in-law's named Joe Cinimon. He was a jeweler who was very valuable to the Nazis because he evaluated all the jewelry they'd stolen from us Jews. This friend of ours Joe had high connections. I told him that Frances and I were illegal here and asked what can be done to have us added to the list. He said he knew a Dr. Fostman, an ear, nose and throat doctor who was with the government of the small ghetto. Joe pleaded with Dr. Fostman to help us girls. He came back saying that Dr. Fostman said he would help but that he was only willing to give permission for one person to stay and that was me. I was supposed to go with him the next day to an office in town to add me to the list. I said, 'Thank-you very much, Mr. Cinimon. But I cannot go without my sister. I will not leave her behind." But he said that he could not change things and the doctor's decision was final. So he wrote a letter allowing Marilla I. Freidenreich to be added to the permitted list for Jews in Radom. I was heartbroken but what could I do?

But then I thought of something I *could* do. Can you tell me the distance between "Marilla I." and "Freidenreich" on a letter? It's a very little space. But I had an idea. I remembered my brother-in-law's sister Esther lived nearby so I went to her apartment and asked for a pen. And in the little bit of space between "Marilla I." and "Freidenreich," I squeezed "Frania" in. It was also very good that "I" in Polish means "and." So now the letter read "Marilla I. and Franya Freidenreich."

By the time I finished it was already 1 or 2 minutes after 5 and the office was closing at 5. I ran as fast as I could to the office with this piece of paper. I squeezed myself the line – it was a long, long line of people who all needed to be added to the quota of Jews who were permitted to stay in the ghetto and not be deported. I pushed my way in the front and yelled out, "I must go in. I have a letter from Dr. Fostman!" I was pushing and pushing my way in front of all the other people who were screaming at me, and I kept saying "I have a letter from Dr. Fostman!"

The woman behind the desk said, "What do you want from me, people? Should I take all of you or should I take instead a letter from Dr. Fostman?" And she took me. Sometimes when the memories come back to me, I close my eyes. I just don't want to remember everything. I wish they would have taken everybody.

So now Frances and I were both legally able to stay in Radom. They had added both of our names to the list. Now that we were legal, the next day Regina went to work and pleaded with the boss in her shop for him to give permission for her to employ us. She came back saying he would allow it but that she could only hire one of us. "Take Frances," I said. And she did.

We were back in Radom for maybe six months before the final deportation in the beginning of 1944. It was winter. Those were hard months but at least I was with what was left of my family. Like I told Mr. Kempner in Blizyn. "What happens to my sisters happens to me. We have to be together."

We did whatever we needed to survive then. Sometimes I would think about the time years earlier after the Nazis came but before we moved to the ghetto when my mother who had come from an important Radom family had gone to her father's grave to cry and say she was sorry that her daughters had to work so hard – my grandfather had wanted so much for his family to be able to live a good life without struggling. But thank G-d all of us had skill with a needle, especially Regina who was so talented that she'd apprenticed with a famous Warsaw dress maker.

Six

TOMASZOW PRISON, AUSCHWITZ, BUCHENWALD

AND LIPSTADT: WINTER, 1944 – SPRING, 1945

In the summer of 1944, when we had been back in Radom for maybe a half year, Regina's husband David lost his job again, this one in the prison where he was working as a guard. If you were an unemployed Jew in the ghetto, you were chased out of town on foot. We had no idea where we were going but we had to stay together. Whatever happened to one of us would happen to all of us! We walked on foot the five of us a long way, we were being marched by the Nazis somewhere but we did not know till we got there that it was a place called Tomaszow Prison. We were there a very short time, probably less than two weeks and we didn't know what they were going to do with us next.

One day they put us on trains and when we got to Auschwitz the first thing they did to us was separate the women from the men. That's when Regina lost herself completely, so worried was she about her husband. He had a bad heart and, although he was good in business, even when they had the book store, she was always the stronger of the two. But now Regina did not know how to save her husband, and without her David she was not the Regina who was in Radom. Also Frances was sick – her typhus had returned the last few months in Radom while she was working for Regina – and she

31

could not help us. I was helping Regina with the child, finding her and all of us food to eat. I was the youngest but I tried hard to grow up overnight.

Without her husband it was like Regina had completely lost her desire to live. "I want to see life again," she told us. "I can't be alone!"

On that first day in Auschwitz we were pushed into a space where they divided us up. "You go first," Regina said to me and Frances. I've thought ever since that it was because she wanted to see us safe that she told us to go first. And then she looked at me and said, "Please be sane, be alert, keep your eyes open." That was the last thing Regina said to me because all of a sudden there was a commotion and she and the baby were pushed with a group of people to the left and Frances and I were called back to go into another line.

The first view of the gates of Auschwitz

But at first I didn't see they were taken to the other line and when I looked back and they weren't there, I said to Frances: "Where are they?"

"They took them away," she said. As soon as I heard that, I started running after them but the watchman pushed me into the barrack. He could have let me go because what did he care? But he didn't. A few minutes later I saw them through the window: Regina in a striped coat. She was holding the child who was wearing a little striped coat. The German pushed me away from the window. I was heartbroken to think I might never see my sister again. Then we were taken to Barrack 18.

Later that day we heard that when they found one woman in line who had hidden her diamond rings in the piece of bread she'd been given. As punishment they took the mothers with children and some of the elderly women in line off to be killed.

I remember that day they took away our clothes so we were all naked, and we were told to carry our shoes in our right hand and our piece of bread in our left hand. I'd filled my boots with woolen scarves I'd made to keep the child warm and entertain her because she'd been restless on the train to Auschwitz and I didn't want her to cry and attract attention. I had also hidden photos of my parents under my arm. We were told to pour water in and out of our shoes to show we weren't hiding anything in them. I just poured a little water in my boots to keep from washing out the wool – the boots were the ones my father had made for me – brown for me, black for Frances. They were going to take away our boots later that day too. That first day in Auschwitz seemed so long but it was just one day. I couldn't swallow a teaspoon of the rice cereal they gave us that night, neither could Frances. I gave it away. I couldn't accept that I would never see Regina again.

I picked the top berth where we all shared one blanket. We heard that night that some of the mothers and children who were taken with Regina and the child were now in Barrack 25 and I quietly slipped out in the middle of the night (if someone had seen me I wouldn't be talking to you now). But Regina and Hadassah were not there. At least Frances was still alive, I told myself. That's how I survived, by having her to watch over. Otherwise there was no reason for me to keep living.

We spent three or four months there working; once Frances had the job of door watcher, letting people in and out. Every morning at roll call they would divide us into lines. One morning they sent me to the left and Frances to the right. I didn't think long, I just ran over to her side thinking that whatever happened to her would happen to me. An ugly red-headed German guard in a uniform caught me with her big hand, and hit me on the breast and back with her whip. She hit me so many times and so hard that I fainted. When I came to, it was already getting dark and I was lying between Barrack 18 and the next one. Ella, a woman who had been a neighbor in Radom, was yelling, "Marilla! Marilla! Marilla!" Why *didn't* they kill me then? I will never know and I will never know who picked me up and dragged me behind the barrack. My sister never told me.

Finally I opened my eyes and I said, "Where am I?" The barracks were empty because they had just deported people. So Ella walked me into Barrack 18. That night there was a large number of Hungarian and Czechs coming into camp. Because the barrack was near the railroad station, from the window I could see could also see a large group of Hungarians arriving. They were well dressed, and the first thing the guards did was take their suitcases. I later heard that they had been told they were going on vacation and to dress for it. Then they moved them into Barrack 18 so it filled up again. Half of this new group they took to the ovens and half they kept as workers.

Jews getting off trains at one of the death camps

After the beating I honestly didn't really care to live, but there was Frances to think about. And remember my brother's wife Liva? She had two brothers, Kalmon and Moshe (Minyk) Baum, very nice guys. And she also had an older sister, Esther (Esthusha) who was with us in Auschwitz too. She was also a very fine person; remember I had gone to her apartment in the ghetto for a pen when I wrote in Frances' name on the form? After Regina was gone, the three of us – Frances and Esther and I — were in Auschwitz together like three sisters.

The next morning at roll call, even though I was so bruised from the beating, I couldn't show any sign that I was in pain or that I'd been beaten. Especially with the camp so full now, I thought they'd take me for sure because I was I was so black-and-blue and my clothing didn't hide all of it. I was also worried they'd take Frances because she was short and still had some signs of her typhus fever. I thought Esther was safe because she was gorgeous.

So what did they do at roll call? They left the two of us alone and took Esther who was so beautiful and strong. But there was no time to think. You just got pushed along. She was so dear to me, like another sister ... but I never saw her again.

That was maybe two days before we had to get our tattoos. I was #65 in line and Frances was #66. We waited a long time in a long line on a very hot day. The tattoo was so painful, every dot hurt. But we knew we couldn't cry out. The number I got that day is still on my arm. Even though it is faded, I can still read it. A-24565.

Every morning there were selections. People you had seen for months all of a sudden you didn't see them anymore. After roll call the ones who weren't selected each got a piece of bread and something to drink.

34

When I think of Auschwitz I also think of my cousin Jacob (Jankiel) Handelsman who was a leader of the plot to bomb the crematoria there. He was a hero, and now he's been made famous in the film *The Grey Zone*. They cut off his pinkie finger before they killed him for being in on the plot.

Sometime late in that year, maybe November, they moved us to Buchenwald. I think we were there a few weeks. We knew they were getting ready to send us somewhere but we didn't know where or why. At Buchenwald, there were always selections, all the time there were selections. Sometimes there they would take half the group out at once.

Then one day 400 of us women were taken from Buchenwald on a long train ride to a munitions factory in Lipstadt, Germany. When we got there, we worked standing up all day long cleaning and polishing bullets and putting them in carts with open tops, two rows in a cart. You were expected to make at least the same amount every day and to do that you had to work very fast. Frances was very good at this. She could do more than they asked. She was getting awards and extra food to eat. And finally they moved her into a different department. I thought, "I'm getting these bullets ready to kill my people and they want me to do more and more." One woman who walked around making sure we were doing our work would pat my hair and every once in a while throw a sandwich in my waste can for me to eat. You would work a certain number of hours and then eat something and sleep. We worked about 12 hours a day and we had to make our numbers or they wouldn't keep us.

Maybe four months later there were a few days when we heard the guards whispering in a way that wasn't ordinary. There were rumors among us too that something was going to happen. We knew that there was something in the air.

Seven

The Death March and Liberation on

the Road: March-April, 1945

After all the years in this or that camp, we never really imagined we would live to see any other kind of life ever again. We had given up on that a long time before this.

But in the camp we kept hearing rumors for the last couple of days and the guards were acting very strange, almost like they were nervous and whispering where we could not hear what they were saying. Some of the Jews said they'd heard the Americans were coming but that was the kind of rumor we had been hearing for so long that we didn't pay attention to it or even hope it could be true.

At the time they were talking about Americans coming we also were hearing that they were planning to take us to Buchenwald to gas us. The Germans seemed to know they were losing the war but still they would have had the greatest pleasure killing us. By doing away with us they would finish the job they set out to do – to destroy us – and it would get rid of the evidence of what they had been doing to us all along.

So we prepared for the worst, but instead of being sent off to die, the guards told us one morning to get ready to march. We had no food or anything that we could take with us but we were told we had to leave. It all just seemed like they had decided this at the last minute. And, before we knew it, they were marching us women out of the camp, really chasing to make us move faster.

Some of the women couldn't keep up and fell away from the group. This had just been too much for them, so as soon as they would fall over, from overwork and thirst and starvation, one of the guards would shoot them. Later I learned that more than 400 of us women made it but I don't know how many began the march, maybe twice that number – those were just the ones of us who lived through those terrible days. On the first night, after a long day of marching with nothing to eat, they pushed us into a barn and locked us in. We had to lie on top of each other so we didn't get much sleep.

In the morning, they marched us again, stopping only once or twice to drink. We were exhausted and hungry and we lost track of the time. But they marched us without food or even much sleep day and night for a week.

The last night we were piled up in a garage, it was really just a big warehouse. But on the morning of the eighth day, instead of marching us, they told us to go into the field next to the warehouse on the outskirts of the town of Kaunitz, and lie down with our faces to the ground in the snow and ice. I remember what it felt like that morning, melting the snow with our bodies and turning everything to mud. Looking back on that day, it seems like the Germans probably heard the sounds of American war planes flying overhead and began to think that they would not be able to get us to Buchenwald in time to have us killed before the Americans get here.

I really don't know how many hours we lay there, probably most of that morning. But lying there we peeked and could see the guards changing from their uniforms into civilian clothes they must have brought with them and running into the woods and toward the town of Kaunitz to try to blend in with everyone else in town. I remember that, even when they had gone, we stayed where we were. We were too afraid to move. Then we heard and felt the ground start to rumble. We didn't know it yet but that was the sound of the American tanks coming toward us.

Until some young boys who'd already been liberated by the Americans ran up to us and yelled, "Women, get up! You are free – the Americans are here!" Still we were frightened. How did we know the guards weren't coming back for us or sending new ones to come and take us? But slowly we got up. We got as much of the mud off of us as we could and we started walking down the road, not knowing where we were going. We saw more and more Jeeps and tanks coming towards us. Thank G-d they belonged to the American soldiers. Since some of the girls in our group knew some English, they spoke with the soldiers. It was Passover and some of the Jewish soldiers had cans of gefilte fish they wanted to give us.

Even though the top guards had changed clothes and run away, some of the lower Nazi guards without civilian cloths had stayed. They just stood there watching us walk away. Some of the women walked back and started to kick some of the guards. I couldn't do it and I didn't do it. But the top Nazi officer bosses had all escaped.

We walked into the town which was Kaunitz, Germany. It was a town that had a large church with a tall steeple. That day it was not just Passover but also Easter Sunday and when we walked into town all the Nazi wives and their children were still in church.

The American soldiers told us to go into the Nazis' homes and not let them back in. I was too afraid to do that. But people we knew, Mrs. Gerover and her daughter Salina – they had owned a pharmacy in Radom – were with us. The mother told me, "You two stay with me. I will take care of you." Another woman, Bronia Slava (everyone called her Branka) walked right into the nicest house in town – it was the banker's house. At first Frances and I along with Mrs. Gerover and her daughter all stayed in a house near the church. But eventually we moved in with Branka and quite a few other women because it was a large house.

We stayed a long time there with the women, several months. Upstairs there were some Hungarian women who brought us chicken and eggs and butter. Frances went with them to get the food from the Nazi stores but I couldn't take it. Once I fell on the steps of the large house we stayed in and hurt my left knee which is still not right and bothers me to this day. By this time the English had already taken over Kaunitz. We were all registered and getting packages from the Red Cross with food and things we needed but had not seen for a very long time like toothpaste, soap and shampoo.

Eight

Life in Kaunitz and a Surprise Visitor, Stuttgart and Marriage: Spring, 1945-1948

I was living with other women in that big fancy house in Kaunitz. Remember Branka, the older woman from Radom who had taken us into the house with her the day we were liberated? I had Frances with me of course and Branka she was not happy about it, but I got her to take a mother and a daughter and two other sisters. There was a lot of room in that house.

I didn't even know how to cook then. My mom was an excellent *bala-bousta*, but not me. Later, after we were married, my husband used to make fun of me. When I cooked rice I cooked it so long it became mush. I tried to bring out the taste I remembered from home but I was never the cook my mother was.

Frances' neck was not right from the day when the Nazis found her working in Regina's shop and beat her because she was working there illegally. Regina was hiding her because Frances' typhus symptoms were back and Regina did not want anyone to find out so she would bring Frances food and penicillin for the typhus. But the Nazis found her and beat her one day when she was working on a sewing machine in the apartment at a time when all the other Jews who worked on the Nazis' things had to go to the bathhouse (every week they had to go so they would be clean to work on their things). Remember I told you that when Regina found out she kissed the Nazis' boots begging them to spare Frances. She told them, "If you kill my sister I will not be able to work!"

Now, how many years later? In Kaunitz, Frances couldn't hold her head straight; she needed a hospital. First she was in a hospital outside the town and she stayed there for several years because it turned out that her vertebrae had been broken from the beating. She was in a body cast for 18 months of that time. I used to go by bus every day to take care of her and feed her. It was a long trip. I made her a little shirt like a baby wears to put over the cast. She had gallstones too from the terrible food we had to eat in the camps and also when they took her out of the cast she could not walk. She needed to learn to walk all over again.

Meanwhile David who was in Italy and on his way to Palestine heard I was alive and in Kaunitz. He had no money but still he managed to cross the Alps. He told the German driver that he had a wife in Kaunitz and that, if he drove him to her, she would pay him. When they arrived, I was so surprised to see him. I remember just standing there gripping a broom and not knowing what to do or say. He came over and kissed me and whispered to me, "Give me money to pay the driver. I'll explain later." I walked into the other room where I kept the ration cards. We had just gotten new ones for the month so I paid him in those. Only my husband could do this and have it work.

I learned more about David in those months after he got to Kaunitz. He was from Kalish, a city in Poland which was not that far from the German border. When the war broke out his parents told him to do whatever he had to do to save himself (he was their only child). So he left there soon after the war began.

David always thought his parents – Meyer and Bayla Kempner – were rounded up with the other Jews of Kalish and sent to the Lodz ghetto and then deported from there to Chelmno where they were killed. David had escaped Kalish before his parents were taken and for a while he was smuggling mostly around Radom, Warsaw, Lublin and Krakow. Remember when he came to my parents' store in the ghetto to pick up his letter? A family named Lassman were his partners; I had gone to school with the Lassmans' little sister. The letter, which was maybe from my cousin Nuta and maybe also from her sister Alla – the two of them knew David from

Warsaw (they lived in the same apartment building) – probably had something to do with the smuggling. Maybe they were warning him not to come back to Warsaw because they had discovered what he'd been up to and were looking for him. He told me later that that he knew it wasn't safe then for him to go back to Warsaw then because at some point the authorities did know what he'd been doing. There was also a time when he had to get away from Radom too for the same reason.

David told me that first he was in the Kielce ghetto and the work camp there. Then he was in Blizyn where you remember we saw each other again for the first time since he came by our place in the ghetto for his letter and he saw my picture of Nuta. He also told me then what he'd been through since Blizyn: the camps at Majdanek, Plasszow and finally Mauthausen-Gunskirchan where the Nazis worked the men very hard breaking up rocks in the quarry. That's where he was liberated from and he was sent to a hospital in Austria and later, with the Jewish Brigade, to Italy. He had a good life there, very good, but he told me the whole time he was there he was determined to find me.

David wanted to take me back to Italy with him but I told him I could not go with Frances still in the hospital. And he said he would not go anywhere without me. When he asked me to marry him, I said, "I can't be a wife to you, I must take care of my sister." And he told me, "As Frances needs you, you need me." He refused to go back to Italy but established himself in Stuttgart and sent me little presents whenever he could.

After Frances had been in the hospital for so long and still she wasn't better, after a while I didn't trust the German doctors in Kaunitz which was run by the British. Stuttgart was run by the Americans and I'd heard it was a better hospital and besides David was there. But the American doctors had not wanted to give me permission to move her there so we got forged papers to let Frances transfer to the hospital from a sculptor friend whose wife was a dentist. He forged the forms as if they were from an American doctor. Dr. Vinepor, a survivor from Radom, was working in the American hospital there. In July 1946, the whole transfer was arranged on the British-run Kaunitz side, a stretcher for Frances, with a chauffeur, a nurse, a doctor and even the British woman who ran the services for the survivors living in Kaunitz. David insisted on paying for the bed in the American hospital in Stuttgart to hold it for her. During the whole trip in the ambulance, I was a nervous wreck. What if they find out the papers are forged? The British woman said to me about David. "Such a man, such a man! You have struggled for so long and here is a good man who wants to take care of you." On that trip to Stuttgart in the ambulance with Frances I decided I should marry him.

But the British woman started flirting with the driver and he wasn't paying attention to the road. So we ran off the road and into the ditch and I was thrown quite a distance. I passed out for a short time and when I woke up I was still in a state of shock. I saw an image of David walking toward me. I thought maybe I had been punished by G-d for not accepting him before this.

By then he was living in an apartment on Bismark Street with a friend, Marian Hoffman. Survivors were given two streets in Stuttgart. I slept in the hospital with Francis. The next morning the English woman said she wanted to find the American doctor who had approved the transfer to thank him! Luckily Marian Hoffman had a car and he and David drove her around showing her the sites of Stuttgart. They kept her busy for so long that they never reached the destination of the hospital. So she had to get home without meeting the doctor!

Then there was the next *tsuris* of trying to register Frances in the hospital since she was there illegally. Plus to get a marriage license. I kept asking myself with my sister in the hospital, who could prepare me for my wedding? I was alone. That time in my life always reminds me of the Yiddish song, *Am I Born from a Stone?*

We ended up having two weddings. The first was with a justice of the peace in my apartment in Stuttgart on July 16, 1946. I still consider that my wedding. My sister was still in the hospital and I didn't want to have a wedding without her. She was the only family I had left. But she was not ready to leave so we stopped at the hospital to get her blessing. Frances and David liked each other a lot and she wanted me to be married. Around that

Our wedding in Stuttgart

42

time one neighbor who'd known David before the war told me, "David Kempner? Not every woman in Kalish could get him." It was a very small and quiet civil ceremony. I wore a red dress and a red hat I had made.

I knew it was at the time compulsory to learn a trade if you were a survivor, so we would not be a burden to the government. But I had kept telling them I had a sick sister in the hospital who I needed to visit every day and it's a long streetcar ride to the hospital. I said I could not work or even train for a job. I would not have the time to do that and still care for my sister.

But after we were married, I was legally in Stuttgart now and had to get work or job training. There was a new ORT school that had just opened there to train survivors for jobs. Sick sister or not, they insisted I join. I said I was handy with a needle. The woman who taught dressmaking (she was from Radom) was having a baby, so they wrote me a letter urging me to be a temporary teacher at the ORT school while she was on maternity leave. My husband said, "Maybe you will get benefits. You have nothing to lose. Take the job." He talked me into it so I went. (There is a picture of me with the students. You can see how many of them are much older than I was then.) To get my diploma I had to go to Munich to take a test. I passed it and from my imagination I created a text to use to teach the class.

Here I am teaching hat-making in the ORT school

After a few weeks of teaching hat-making, they really respected me and I didn't mind the work. I was asked to begin giving the students an examination and signing the working papers for them saying they could do this work in America or Israel.

Then the other teacher came back from maternity leave and none of the students wanted her; they all wanted me. She came into my class and embarrassed me, saying the eggs are no smarter than the chicken. I came home crying and told my husband I was very uncomfortable with the situation.

43

The school wanted to keep both of us but she didn't want that. She wanted her class back and said she didn't want to stay under the circumstances. But she eventually accepted it and they opened up another class for her so we each kept our own classes.

By this time, Frances was doing alright but she still wasn't well enough to come home. There was a man named Weinberg from my town who introduced me to the professor in his medical school in Heidelberg. The professor said if he would make a special trip to examine her in the hospital he would have to charge a fortune but he said that in a few weeks he had to be in Stuttgart anyway and he would come to examine Frances then. He came and examined her and said he would leave word to accept her in his clinic in Heidelberg. I had to find transportation for her but we finally got her there. She was there for a while then transferred to a convalescent center in a castle, Schloss Elmau. That's where she really learned to walk again.

By this time David had started talking about going to America but I didn't want to go anywhere until we could have a real Jewish wedding. So more than two years after our first one with the justice of the peace, we invited everyone we knew to come to our apartment on August 16, 1948. I had a pink dress custom-made for me at ORT and I made a hat with a short veil. If you look at the picture of us, you can see my husband's cousin Sasha Katz on the left side – her son would be Irv's college roommate someday.

Newlyweds: David and me in Germany

We brought my sister out of the hospital for the wedding (That was when she was still in Heidelberg). I remember Frances had the bedroom and David and I slept in the living room. But she got sick again after the wedding. Starches weren't digesting properly.

A few months later, after Frances had been moved to the convalescent center, we had an offer from ORT to go to Israel so I could teach there. But, even though they promised to send Francis to join us there when she was better, I could not leave my sister there alone so I said no.

It was now 1948 and the two-and-a-half years we had lived in Stuttgart were mostly good ones. Frances finally got out of the convalescent center and moved in with us. I was teaching and David was in the clothing business, even then, buying and selling. Since we hadn't gone to Israel with ORT and since neither of us had any family left in Poland, we started to think more seriously about America and David began to spend a lot of his time writing to friends and fellow survivors who were already in North America to see how we could get there too.

Nine

WE BEGIN LIFE IN AMERICA: 1949-1964

My husband had a friend, Manny Duell, who came to the US in the 1930s, marrying the granddaughter of one of the wealthiest Jews in Poland, Poznanski. He owned land, stores and factories. But many years before the war Poznanski sold off his fortune in Poland and moved to America.

"Could you send us papers saying you are my cousin?" I wrote for David. "Whatever it costs, we are both willing to work hard to pay you back."

Manny wrote back to David, "Don't think you will have an easy life here. I remember you were an only child and not used to hard work." Then we wrote back: "I am different now. I lived six years under the Nazis. I am now a hard worker." Also we wrote that David now has a wife and she has sister who he is responsible for. We did not write that the sister had been sick. But it takes so much time to legalize everything that, even after Manny agreed to sign for us, the whole process took many, many months.

Finally after so many papers and documents had to be signed and sent, we got a letter telling us to go for a medical exam. I dressed my sister nicely and put rouge on her cheeks so she would look healthy.

The trip over to America on the ship seemed to last forever and my sister was throwing up the whole time. We left from Remenhofen, Germany in late February, 1949 and we were on the ship for two weeks. By the time we got into New York it was March 11.

We arrived at night and I kept asking if someone named Duell might have come for us. I didn't know that one of the people who had met the ship had been his brother-in-law, his sister's husband, not a Duell. But he didn't find us. Still, no one seemed to come for us as far as we knew so we were still there in the morning.

We arrive in America

My sister was still vomiting and I was pushing her on the deck in a wheelchair. David was standing in line to get our baggage. I was upset. Where will we go? There was a woman from HIAS or the Joint who patted me on the hair and said in Yiddish, "Don't cry. You are among Jews. You are in good hands!" By then there was nobody left, just a few people who'd come for their cargo. The lady said, "Are you sure you have nobody? There is a fancy lady who just came asking for you. *Shmek gelt* – tastes like money."

When I asked this lady who came looking for us (I had learned a little English in Stuttgart) "Whom do I have the pleasure?" she just said, "I am here on Mr. Duell's behalf." It turned out to be Mrs. Duell, but she did not want anyone to know who she was. She put us in a taxi and told the driver to take us to the Chesterfield Hotel near Radio City Music Hall and to book us two rooms. But I said no, we only need one room. The only money we had was the G-marks from my teaching at the ORT school which I'd sewn into my clothes. I also told her that we would only let them pay for the first week. My sister was not well when we arrived and had been throwing up and in the ship hospital during the trip. And I said we needed to find her a hospital. But Mrs. Duell said, "She's just tired. She'll be alright," and to the driver, "Take them to the hotel." It was $35 a night which was a lot of money then and a lot of money especially for us.

I remember the hotel served us grapefruit. I had never even seen grapefruit before. I thought: It is so sour but so expensive. When they gave it to me the second time I said in the English I knew, "Thank you very much but I don't want you to spend your time." I remember also I had a thermos of water because my cold was so severe and we paid $2 for a thermos of water in the hotel. My sister was throwing up in the hotel that night. My husband

47

insisted on paying for everything and by the end of five days we had nearly nothing left. Duell's sister's husband came to see us at the hotel that night. When I told him we were nearly out of the money we brought, he said, "Go to HIAS and let them help you."

The next day, we went, by taxi because we didn't know any better then. I knew only that my sister was sick and needed a hospital. The people at HIAS told us that we had to rely on Duell until we get on our feet. My husband whispered to me, "Don't you understand? He just did us a favor by saying we were blood relatives."

The Duells who sponsored us as immigrants to America

But the HIAS man was like a wall. "Mr, Duell brought you here and he is *shmek* with *gelt.*" He got so mad, my husband, and he says, "I am not asking for anything for us, my wife and I will take any kind of work. Just take my sister-in-law to the hospital." He was so angry he grabbed the heavy crystal inkwell on the man's desk. I was afraid he was going to throw it at him. So the man gave us a letter to admit Frances to Mt. Sinai Hospital. The next day I was sick also and I kept hearing the Yiddish song in my head, *Tell Me Where I Should Go*. Back at the hotel, when the woman at the front desk saw me she sent for a doctor. He came to the room, a Jewish doctor from Poland. And he wanted to send me to the same hospital as Frances. Then there was a knock on the door and it was Mr. Duell! I am in the bed and not in nice shape. He just gotten back from Paris – he could speak Polish and like I said, I could speak a little English, so I told him that Frances was in the hospital.

He was friendly and before he said good-bye he invited us for dinner at their home at 29 Fifth Avenue. I said to David, "Go by yourself." But he said, "You must go. I will not go by myself." We had our clothes in a storage room and my husband found a suit for him and a dress for me. He paid for a tailor to iron his suit and we took another taxi to Fifth Avenue.

What a home! What a place! The first thing I saw was a crystal table with crystal legs, with doilies on it. And a black woman in a black uniform with a white apron and another one who was the maid. Manny said to us, "Do you know the dress my wife is wearing cost $1,200?" They served something that I later learned was barley mushroom soup but I was afraid to open my mouth because I had such a bad cold and the phlegm was choking me. The wife doesn't touch anything, only the help serves us. My husband takes a taste of something but it doesn't taste right he says to me. "*Vas is dus*?" he asks Mr. Duell. "It's good," he says. "It's called shrimp." My husband pushed it away. "I won't eat it," he said.

That night Manny told us there was a meeting coming up in New Jersey of people from Kalish, mostly in the embroidery business, which Kalish was famous for, and would we like to go? "Then more people will know you are here and be able to help you," he said. Manny drove us to the meeting, and we crossed the George Washington Bridge which was such a sight. We got there and everyone was so happy to see David and I wondered, who are these people with such friendly faces?

"Dovid, Dochu, where were you?" two fancy ladies were calling to him. They were two sisters, Sadie Diament and Mary Smullen, David's second cousins! Their parents had come to America before the war and they owned the United Embroiderers Factory in New Jersey. Later they had come back to Kalish and lived in the same building as David's family but when the war broke out they were able to leave because they were already American citizens, so during the burnings and gassings they were already here. Another sister Rose was living in France. I visited them in France years later. The whole family was very wealthy. They were not kosher but they were crazy about David. "You go home," they said to Manny. "We will take them back to the hotel." Apparently they took a liking to me too and dropped us off late that night.

The next day they were back at our hotel offering me a ride to the hospital to visit my sister. Then they took us back to Mary's house in Fort Lee, New Jersey. What a home! The next day they sent a truck from the factory and picked us and all our things and took us to an apartment in New Jersey. But Duell said he also felt responsible for us and offered David a job on Madison Avenue, cutting the material for ladies underwear. It was good for him to work but it was a long trip from New Jersey every day.

We were there maybe a little more than a month when David met with a man he had known in the camps who seemed to have sort of a debt he owed David. David was a very likable man, as I already said. This man was David Goembersky, only now he had shortened it to Glen. He also had a factory in New Jersey, not a big one but he made a living. He began inviting us to his home in New York on 163rd Street in Washington Heights. He and his wife Irene remembered that I had given them my bedroom when they visited us in Stuttgart.

Beginning life anew in America

And a few short weeks after we met the Glens we moved to 162nd Street in Washington Heights which was near them and closer to our jobs. Because I had also gotten a job by then. I found it when I was looking through the ads in the Jewish newspaper, *Aufbau*, which means "builds up from nothing." There was an ad looking for a hat maker for a factory in the Bronx which made hats for Saks Fifth Avenue and other nice stores. Before that I was doing knitting and crocheting at home for pennies.

The boss Mark Schwartz right away put me to work on the important hats. We each had our part of the table to work on and, being handy with a needle, I picked it up quickly. I knew I had to learn fast. When his manager came back to work a few days later she could see I knew what I was doing when she saw he had put a few of my hats on the hat stands. Somehow I was good at it, better than good I must say. And she did not like that at all. She came at 11 that morning and saw what I had done in just a couple of hours – we were paid by the number of hats we made, not by the hour. She slid her finger under my stitches and told the boss that I make stitches for dead bodies, that they were too big. I stood up and said I was a newcomer to this country (he spoke to us in German) and, if she will continue to touch my hats, I will leave. I knew my work was good and that he had praised it. He appeased me and said, "Marilyn, forget about that and go ahead and keep working." I came home crying that night. I would have quit but we needed the money.

For more than four years until her wedding Frances was with us. She had the second bedroom and we turned the dining room into a bedroom for Irv who was born in 1950. When she married, he moved into his own room. In the early years in Washington Heights when Frances had just gotten back from gall bladder surgery, she had been told to take it easy and just do a little cooking for a while. But one day she said to me, "If you don't find me a job, I am going to end up back in the hospital!" I asked my boss to help because he sold our hats to Saks Fifth Avenue and I knew they had an alterations department. Frances was good with a needle too, like me and like Regina.

I didn't realize it then but the truth is I needed someone to take care of. If I didn't have Frances all those years I would have wanted to die like the rest of my family. I really didn't care to live especially after they took Regina and the child. I remember my friend, Lola Marcus, the only daughter of a famous tailor in Radom. She was raised as a princess. I ran into her on the street named after Marie Curie many years earlier. I always remember that she was the one who told me to watch over Frances. "She is very sick," she told me. I heard she survived. We ended up in the same barrack and bunk in Auschwitz. It was strange that somehow in the night people changed places and we often wound up sleeping with people we had known from before.

In 1949 I had a breast cancer scare. I was having pain in the breast where the red-headed Nazi guard had beaten me. But didn't want to spend the money on a doctor. "Go, we'll pay," David said. "It's a cyst," the doctor said. "You need a biopsy." But after everything I'd been through I did not want them to cut me open. I wanted to die whole. So I told him no biopsy. "Well, if you get pregnant, it might go away," he said. I had never thought about pregnancy. We had been married for many years by now and I didn't think I wanted a child. Look, my sister, Regina, had a child and in the end they both died. Now Francis was working and David and me too. I was making hats that sold for $140 not $3, and I was earning three times what he was.

But I did get pregnant. When the boss noticed me getting bigger, he said, "Marilyn, how could you do something like this? You could have made a career here." I said, "Mr. Schwartz, as soon as the child is born, I will get a maid." I was taking English classes with Frances at night so my English was improving. Later she also finished high school. I wanted her to polish herself and she made some wonderful friends.

I found a German Jewish woman who lived a few blocks away who said she would take care of the baby so I could go back to work. I worked as long as I could. Irv was born on July 30, 1950. It was a difficult birth. I was too weak to go down for the bris. The Glens were there and the Duells came too, and David's New Jersey cousins the Diaments and the Smullens. Irene Glen came to see me and told me to call him Irving. She couldn't have children. I think in the paper he's Isaac. But it should have said Yitzhak after my dad. He was a big baby and a gorgeous baby as all the nurses kept telling me.

I went back to work after a while. And the German Jewish woman started to watch him. One day there wasn't enough work and we got off early. I was home by 12. When I entered the building I heard a child screaming and I said, "It sounds like my boy." I opened the door with a key and peeked into the kitchen where she was squeezing oranges and cooking for herself. Then I see my son in the crib screaming and playing with his doody. I said to myself that I will not go to work anymore if this is what is happening to my child, even though I was making far more money than David was making with Duell. That night I said, "Mr. Kempner I am not going to work anymore." He said, "Why?" I told him what happened and said, "No one will take care of my child but me, and whatever you make will have to be enough. We'll manage. He didn't come to me so easy and I am not going to let him be neglected. He's named after my father."

I fixed, I knitted. We managed. Duell raised David to $50 a week. Till 1954 when she got married and moved to New Jersey, Frances was still with us and she helped out too. She used to put money on the table. I saved up that money for her wedding but sometimes I had to use it for bills. That's how it was, what can I tell you?

Frances developed such confidence at that job. She became a floor lady at Saks and started dating and bringing boys home to meet us. I tried to play the role of her mother, even though she was six years older than me.

In 1952 when Irv was 2 we moved from 505 162nd Street up the street to 659 and into a bigger place. It was a beautiful apartment. One of Frances' dates came by to pick her up and said, "It looks like Truman lives here!"

One night in May of 1953, David could not sleep. I kept hearing the door opening and shutting and I saw him putting his head out the open window to get some fresh air. He was usually a good sleeper but that night he had been pacing back and forth. In the morning, it was a Saturday and our usual doctor was religious so I went down to the corner and found another doctor to come and see David. "Something is wrong," he said. "He has to see a neurologist." The next morning our regular doctor said David had to go the hospital. Irv, who was not yet 3, was bouncing up and down in his crib. I said, "Honey, please behave. Daddy has to go to the hospital."

"Popsicle? Hopsicle!" he sang. "Give him medicine, Give him the whole jar!"

I took Irv to friends on 164th Street and another friend came with me when I took David to the hospital. The decision was made that he needed brain surgery and they told me it was a very dangerous operation. I had the European mentality that you would sell the last pillow in the house if necessary to get the biggest doctor and the best hospital. The Duells recommended him. I did not ask this big doctor how much it was going to cost to do the operation. The New Jersey cousins (the two sisters) were very well-to-do and, even though they were only second cousins, they were very involved with us. They liked David and they liked me. I was very grateful. I borrowed $1,000 from them, of course he charged much more, plus the hospital bill.

After the surgery was successful, the doctor told me how much it was going to cost me. "Why didn't you tell me you couldn't pay?" he said. "If he was the king of England we couldn't have done any more for him!" I went back to work at the hat factory to pay the cousins back and the rest of the bills. And I made a beautiful dinner for them the night we paid them back.

David went to a convalescent home for a few weeks after the surgery. Then I asked the cousins who had a big summer house in New Jersey, more like a hotel, if he could spend the summer there. The doctor had told me that David had (G-d forbid) a weak heart and should never work full-time again or take public transportation, so I wanted him to be somewhere quiet. I remember it was also a very hot summer in the city. I kept

Irv and me in New York

53

asking myself what my parents would do if they were in my situation. And how I can spare Irv from a bad situation to grow up in.

You asked me about the business. It started after David's brain surgery. Another survivor, Isaac Rosen, came to us in New York and told me that his mother had sent him to me. She had told him, "Marilla will make a mensch of you!" since he was an only child and a little spoiled. He knew me already very well because I had kept him when his mother had the typhus in the camp.

David was still in the convalescent home when Isaac came and I didn't think he was going to be able to go back to work at Duell's. So I asked Isaac, "Would you like to go into business with my husband?" He said, "Do you mean it?" I said, "Yes, but first he has to get well." David did not go back to work for Manny after his surgery, so when he got better the two of them opened KeRo Lingerie in a shabby neighborhood. I was unable to work at this time but took in sewing and knitting and borrowed money from his New Jersey cousins Sadie and Mary to live. And we had to use more of the money Frances was giving us from her job. It took a while to set things up so the business didn't really start till right after Frances' wedding. And then it took even longer for the business to succeed. But it did.

When he got home from the convalescent home, David was bored and restless – he had to lie on his stomach for three months. That was before the business really began. Maybe throwing himself into the business also helped my husband recover because he began slowly to come back to himself again. David loved to dance, and tell jokes. He was entertaining. Everyone loved him. And so smart – he would read everything he could get his hands on.

By then it was 1954 and I was back at the hat factory and Frances had left Saks to be floor lady at another factory. That was also the year she married Joey Zurawin, a survivor from Warsaw. She bought Irv his suit for the wedding. He was turning 4 that year. She was 38 and Joey was maybe a year or two

Irv and me with some Smullen and Diament cousins

younger. His father Yaakov who everyone called Pop tended to the geese and chickens on their farm until he died in 1979. But Joey's mom and sisters had been killed.

This is how they met: Frances had a friend from Bais Yaakov who lived on a farm in Vineland, New Jersey and she would visit her there. Their neighbors were Joey and his father who also had a farm. After the wedding, Frances moved there and opened a business selling women's lingerie and other clothing in the basement of their house (she got a lot of her stock through our family's connections in the garment business).

Frances' marriage was a happy one. She was also a hard worker and a successful businesswoman. A real *ballibusta*. But she wasn't able to have children. I think her body had been through too much from the camps.

After a while the commute to the Bronx was killing me. I was taking several buses to get home at night. I tried for a while to work for a woman who had a clothes and hat store who needed someone to fix hats. But she was an anti-Semite and that job lasted only a little while. Other jobs I had were as a saleslady in a department store and for a while at the offices of social security. Whatever I did I always put my whole self into it.

Meanwhile for several years the business had been going well. But one day in 1959 I noticed a little dot on David's back and then saw how fast it was growing. At one point he even had a suit jacket made to fit over it because soon it was like a grapefruit. The doctors found it was cancerous. It was another difficult surgery. I remember they would not let Irv up to see his father because he was only 9 and hadn't turned 13 yet. He stood on his tiptoes to try to look taller so he could see his father.

David was four months between the hospital and the convalescent home. While he was recuperating in Columbia Presbyterian, I had minor skin surgery and told the doctor I had not had my menstruation for a while. He gave the test and I thought: What will I do if I *am* pregnant with a husband in the hospital recovering from back surgery and a 9-year-old to care for? Nothing was normal in my life. Everything had big obstacles. When I told David that I was pregnant, at first he was so sad because he did not expect to live to see it. "When you have the baby you will name it after me," he said. But he lived and he absolutely adored Tes and she adored him.

But in 1959 people I knew including one doctor kept telling me to "get rid of" it since I had been through so much already and had a sick husband

and another child. "How will you manage?" they said. I knew what that meant: to have an abortion. But I would not even consider taking the life of my child. Also I kept thinking that if something happens to us at least Irv will have someone in this world: a sibling. I remember I was bleeding but I didn't want to lose this pregnancy. I remember Irv saying, "Mommy, don't worry. I will take care of you!"

And such miracles happened. I had nobody but still people helped. At one point during my pregnancy my cousin from Radom, Stanley Handelsman who lived in Australia by then, took me and Irv to Canada for a rest and to see his sister my cousin Manya.

When Tes was born on May 27, 1960, after all my worrying, she was perfect and so beautiful. When the nurse asked me what I would be calling her, I started to cry and said, "I will name her for my mother."

As a child Tes was already bright and funny. I was able to dress her beautifully too. Everyone commented on her beauty and how charming she was always. Even as a small child she was a performer and a comedienne. When Tes was 3, my cousin Stanley's brother Moshe came to visit and she was outraged. "Why do you call him *Feteh* Moshe?" (Feteh means 'uncle' in Polish). He's not fat!" By the way, this is the same Handelsman family who was related to Jacob Handelsman or as we called him Jankiel, one of the heroes who blew up one of the crematoria in Auschwitz.

I remember that this Moshe also came all the way from Israel (he was one of the men who started the Egged bus company there) to be

Tes and me

at Irv's bar mitzvah in 1963. We still called him Feteh Moshe. It's also interesting that his daughter Judy moved to America after she finished with the Israeli army, to Queens not far from our house with her husband Sam Mayer. He was a successful textile engineer. Judy only had one child, Shelly, who grew up to marry Noah Sokolow. Now they own two of the biggest kosher restaurants in Teaneck, New Jersey: Shelly's and Noah's Ark Deli.

Meanwhile our good friends the Glens had moved to Rego Park in Queens with their adopted son and they kept telling us to come too. They said the other half of their house – they were side-by-sides – was going to be available but not for a few years, so we gave them $4,000 to put down on it, money we had gotten from the Germans as reparations. But when they found out I was pregnant with Tes, the Glens cooled towards us.

Three years later, in 1962, they told us the house would come available in the next two years. By this time David wanted not to live near them anymore because they no longer wanted anything to do with us. But I reminded him that at first we didn't want to accept the bloody money from the Germans either but that this money was going to allow us to have the house and the neighborhood our children need. I knew that Irv would be able to go to a better high school in Queens than in Washington Heights and I wanted better for Tes too.

Meanwhile with David recovering, Isaac told me, "When he's ready to come back to work we're not going to let him work so hard." But one night my cousin Stanley

Celebrating Irv's bar mitzvah with David, the children and my sister Frances

Handesman came over and said he had gone to see the business. "Why do trust him? Why not go see it for yourself?" he said to me. He said something wasn't right there.

Even when our neighbor Felicia (who was related to Isaac's wife) told me that she heard Isaac was embezzling funds, and I told my husband who was still in the convalescent home, he said, "Felicia is *mashugah*." David did not want to believe it since he and Isaac had been such good friends as well as business partners. But he realized little by little that something wasn't kosher with the business. Isaac it turned out had been taking money from the business that wasn't his to take for probably years. When he found out, my husband didn't ever want to see him again.

57

In the end David got something from the business, but not what he should have gotten. They dissolved the business and sold off the equipment and the inventory. The business had lasted for 10 years in all, 1953 to 1963 when Tes was still very little. And, even though he wasn't completely well yet, David and I decided he should go to school to learn to become a stockbroker.

Ten

OUR LIFE IN QUEENS: 1964-1999

The Glens had our $4,000 for quite a few years as down payment on the other half of their house in Rego Park in Queens. But by the time we actually completed the sale and moved in there were a lot of hard feelings between us. And for a while they had been telling us that they wanted to give us back our $4,000 with interest.

My husband wanted to take back the $4,000 since they were behaving badly and even though we had been such good friends. David didn't even want to see them much less live in the same building as them, right across the wall. He went to the lawyer's office to sign the paper releasing them from our purchase agreement and giving us back our money with interest. After he left for the lawyer's office my friend Hutka came over and I told her what he was doing. She said, "You are allowing this to happen? Don't let him do it!" She was right. The neighborhood we lived in was becoming less Jewish and I wanted that house for the children to have better schools and a better place to grow up. As beautiful as our apartment was in Washington Heights, I knew Queens was better for us and Tes could have her own room instead of being in a crib in our room. Also it would belong to us, not to a landlord with us just throwing away rent money each month.

So I called the office and asked to speak with David. "Don't sign that paper," I said. "I changed my mind. I want that house." After he hung up he said to the Glens, "No deal."

We moved in 1964, the same year Manny Duell died of a heart attack after diving into a pool. Tes was 4 when we moved and Irv 14 so she was able to start school there and he was able to start high school. I missed Washington Heights for two or three months – Queens was so different. But we joined the Rego Park Jewish Center and got involved there and I began to like it and feel at home. I lived there for almost 50 years!

Our family on our front porch in Queens with friends from Poland

After we moved in, the Glens wanted to make up but David felt that they had tried to cheat us out of buying the other half of their home so he never spoke to them again. But they had such *tsuris* with their adopted son that I felt badly for them. They built a high brick wall between our two front porches. Eventually they moved to New Jersey and a nice survivor family moved in.

Many years later we ran into Irene at a bungalow colony and she said, "Davshu! How are you?" I pleaded with him to talk to her because when you don't speak to someone who has hated you then you are doing as much wrong as they are. And what they went through with that son, it was terrible. When I thought about everything they had done for us after the brain surgery, I know could not have made it if it weren't for them. I spoke to her but David, he would not speak to her. He had been too hurt.

They called David the *wonderkind*. First he recovered from such dangerous brain surgery and was still so smart and then from widespread cancer on his back. After finding out about Isaac and then the business folding, he started again, going to school to be a stockbroker. And he was a good one. He always had a good business head and people trusted him. Irv used to go to his father's office as a boy and he learned a lot from him. He also has a terrific business head like his father. David was happy then. People looked up to him and came for his advice. As survivors we were beginning to get monthly payments from the Germans, a pension after so much hardship. Plus with what David was making and with our social security we could make it.

Meanwhile the children were growing up. When he was in the Forest Hills High School, a very good school, Irv had a tendency to go to bed late, wake up late, take a quick shower and leave the house with wet hair, even in the winter. And no matter how I begged him, he would not wear a hat. So I was constantly getting calls from the high school that he was sick and to come pick him up and take him home. So, when it came time to pick a college, I told him, "If you really want to go away, the only place I would send you is Florida since then I wouldn't have to worry about you getting sick." But when he got there he had a terrible problem with an anti-Semite of a roommate and one day Irv called me saying "If you don't get me out of here, I am going to kill him." I had to go to Florida and somehow was able to switch him to the room of Jay Katz. Jay's mom June Katz was a student of mine after the war in the ORT school in Germany. And she was at our wedding. Now all those years later, Irv and her son became college room-mates and you know what? Today they are still friends.

Tes was a very good student. Her first day of kindergarten when I came to pick her up, there she was holding the teacher's hand. The teacher said, "Mrs. Kempner, your daughter just became president of the class." That was Tes always: smart and confident. She taught me not to be afraid of other people. She was always singing, even as a child. I remember her singing *Summertime* from *Porgy and Bess*. I also taught her to say "Who has such a sweet face?" in Polish.

"I do!"

"Who taught you?"

"My mother!"

"Do you love your mother?"

"Yes!"

"Why do you love your mother?"

"Because she is good!"

It was amazing. She was so young but she learned it so easily and she still remembers it! Her father was crazy about her. I remember after his brain surgery he would hold her on his lap. He had a big scar up his fore-head and holding her made him very happy. He loved her so much.

Both of the children are so smart. Irv didn't study so hard. He'd just study at the last minute and still get good marks. When Tes used to work at the bank they told me she's not only beautiful, she has a *kup* – a head on her shoulders. David's illness was very hard on Tes, who was just a child. She loved him so much and missed him when he was not around, she was lost without him. After two years of college in Florida, I said to Irv, "You are going to have to find a school in New York. I can't handle Tes and your father by myself." He came home for a short time having already accepted a job at a camp in Florida. Then he transferred to New York University and Mindy who was from Florida came too. She went to NYU in the Bronx and much later Tes went to Queens College. After a little while Irv and Mindy got married – he was 20 and she was 19. I had to sign for him because he was too young to get married without it. They rented an apartment but then they went to Israel for a while before having children.

A few years later I also took Tes to Israel. She was 12 then. There were so many people there from Radom and many others from David's family who managed to survive. Over the years many of them who came to America would stay in our house.

David retired from his stockbroker job at 62; he had no strength left. And in 1985 Joey died of Lou Gehrig's disease. I remember we were walking into the house from Yom Kippur services when the phone was ringing. It was Frances saying Joey had died. I think it was a Thursday. The next day at the funeral David wasn't feeling well so he went back to New York and I stayed for the *shiva* with Frances so she shouldn't be alone. In New Jersey Joey had a lot of family so for a while she had people around her. But after a while she sold the farm for very little to Joey's family. She said it was important to her to leave a good name with the family there. That's when Frances moved back up to New York and I helped her buy an apartment near us so my children were able to spend some time with her. She stayed close to us the rest of her life. Frances lived another 22 years after Joey died. She died in 2007.

After Irv got married, he stayed at NYU and then got a sales job with Gillette. For a while the company moved him around a lot and when Mindy was pregnant, he won a trip to Israel. They saw Feteh Moshe there maybe a few years before he died.

When Sarah Batyah was born in 1977, I became a grandmother for the first time. Then again when Benjay was born in 1979, and Jeremy in

1981. My three grandchildren have always been special to me ever since they were babies. Jeremy as a child always liked my mushroom-barley soup. I remember something he once said to me. "See that house, Grandma? Someday I will grow up and buy it and you will live with me!"

"What will you do for a job?" I asked him.

"The same thing my daddy does!" he said. In his smile he reminds me so much of my father. Batyah and Benjay are also very warm whenever they see me. Batyah has five of her own now and Benjay has four and now Jeremy has a baby too.

One day near the end of January, 1999 when he was 88, David collapsed in the bathroom. We were waiting for the taxi to take us to the airport to go to Miami Beach where we had a place. He'd had a heart attack. He made it to the hospital in the ambulance. But once in the hospital he developed pneumonia and his heart was too weak to take the strain. He died two days later on January 25.

Irv and Mindy were on a business trip then in Puerto Rico, our grandson Benjay was on his way home from a year studying in Israel and our granddaughter Batyah had to fly in from Wisconsin where she was in college. Tes was in a hospital in Los Angeles recovering from the flu but she came anyway, and everyone in the family was back in time for David's funeral.

Eleven

Where I Am Now and What I Have Learned

It's very tough to live with my memories, very tough.

When I can't sleep I think about the home I came from. We weren't rich but I had everything I needed and whatever obstacle we faced I knew we would pull through. I know when I wanted to stay home that day right before the second deportation and my mother insisted I go to work and walked me to the pick-up place, that she did it because she wanted to save me. She saved my life that day because if I had stayed home they would have taken me along with my parents. And since my mom saved me, I was able to save Frances. In the end, she was able to have a very good life. She never worried about anything even in the worst times.

My parents didn't have to tell me to be a good person. I just watched them. It was because of them that I always wanted to save the people I loved. If I had a purpose in my life, it was to help. But I know that if I didn't come from the home I did I would not have made it. Knowing that there is a G-d, that with your birth he sends you your life package, the good and the bad. There was Shabbat and the holidays, and the way my parents spoke at home, these are all part of my survival. No matter how bad things got I always knew I was a somebody. I was their child. When I remember where I came from I can tolerate anything.

You asked what happened to our family. Did you know that my husband's father Meyer was a strong Zionist and his brother-in-law, Udel

Wolkovitch, my mother-in-law's brother, was part of the fourth *aliyah* to Israel from Poland after the First World War? It was a very hard life then but he convinced my father-in-law (who of course I never met) to visit, hoping he would also move there. My father-in-law went sometime around 1928 or 1929, leaving David with his mom Bayla.

For a while my father-in-law worked on a kibbutz and he was captured while he was on guard duty and tortured by the Arabs. They cut off a toe and left him a written message: "Jew, go back to the safety of Poland. You are not wanted here." So that's what he did, but he and Bayla were taken from their home in Kalish just a few years later to the Lodz Ghetto and when that was liquidated probably they were killed in the Chelmno concentration camp with other Lodz Jews.

We found out more about what had happened to both our families and our friends from the other survivors we met through the Kalish and Radom Mutual Societies. It was at one of the meetings of the Kalish group that something amazing happened. The speaker was a woman named Hannah Vardemon who was talking to us about some of the JNF projects that were needing money for Israel. Her husband and little boy were there too and he kept pointing at David. He told his father that David looked just like his grandfather, Hannah's dad. When my husband asked who Hannah's dad was, it turned out it was my husband's uncle, his mother Bayla's brother Udel who had remained in Israel and not returned with Meyer to the "safety" of Poland!

Did you also know that when I met David he was an only child, but that he once had a younger brother named Berel? He was 4, when a Polish doctor gave him an overdose of a drug when he was being treated for some sort of illness. Just like I once had a sister named Channa who also died at 4.

My mother had a large family and hardly any of them survived but there were a few of her sister Chava's children who did. They were cousins – the Moshoviches – but growing up we were closer than that. My uncle Moshovich had a famous brother, Rabbi Moshovich. Chava's husband started a fabric business and changed his name to Moss and became very wealthy. His mother and my mother they loved each other so much. Regina was very close their kids in Warsaw including Chava's daughter Nuta who also survived the war and lived in Paris. Their brother Jermiya – Jerry – also survived.

But during the war he (Jerry) was drafted by the Polish army along with Nuta's bridegroom. She was pregnant then and a few months after the war broke out she had a baby boy. The goyim gave her a non-Jewish name and got her a job in an office. In the church, using the baptism papers of a dead parishioner, to save the boy they gave him a goyish name and listed him as Catholic. One day she came home from work and the boy was gone; they had given him away. I don't know what became of him.

Nuta survived as you know but her champion swimmer husband who'd been taken by the Polish army with her brother Jerry, she believed did not survive. But one day after the war in Warsaw in the street Nuta's husband met a mutual friend who asked if he had seen Nuta. He didn't know she was alive and had gotten married again. His new wife was pregnant but still he wanted to divorce his new wife and go back to Nuta. Nuta told me that maybe if the wife had not been pregnant she would have taken him back but not now. Nuta then married Mr. Dornbusch, a man who she didn't love but he threatened to commit suicide if she didn't. They lived in Paris. But she never had any more children. She was 10 years older than me, Regina's age. I heard that many years later that her first husband and his family went to Israel but on his bed-stand he kept Nuta's picture always.

There was also their sister Karolla of course. She ran away to Russia when they were bombarding Warsaw and married a survivor and moved to Toronto where she raised two daughters Eva and Sarah who are both married with children of their own now. And her brother Marcel Beam (he changed his name from Moshovich) went to France and worked for HIAS and then to England – he smuggled himself across the English Channel. And there he came across an English woman named Doris, very pretty, and they married and had a boy two or three years younger than Irv. Their son, Rodger, worked for a newspaper in England, maybe now he's a publisher in England.

Marcel came to see us in New York after my husband's brain surgery. He told me how much he loved my mother. Doris told me, "I'm sorry to say this but if this hadn't happened I would never have met my husband." My cousin said, "Marilla, how do you like my shiksa?" She got angry and said, "I don't call you a dirty Jew!"

Irv looks a lot like my brother David and Jeremy reminds me a little of my brother, something in his smile. My brother was such a warm guy, people loved him. Jeremy is like him in that way too.

Irv is Yitzhak Meyer, named after both the grandfathers who would never meet him. Tes is named for her grandmothers, my mother Tirza and my mother-in-law Bayla. And one of my great-granddaughters, Rayna Hadassah, is named after my sister, Regina, and little Hadassah who were killed in Auschwitz.

Being good with a needle saved me and my sisters too so many times. Did you know that when she was only 18 or 19 Regina was already training in dressmaking in Warsaw and working in the fancy place where my Aunt Masha had her clothes made? She was so talented, and when she came back to Radom she was her own boss making very fine dresses. For me, I mostly made hats, who knows how many thousands in my lifetime? Though I also worked some times in department stores, a photo studio, for other smaller shops and in the social security office for a while. And I always took in crocheting, knitting and alterations which I did for many years especially while the kids were growing up.

As a family we were not just passable. My cousin Jankiel Handelsman who I remember as such a nice guy growing up and smart too was killed for doing something very courageous. He was part of the sondercommndo at Auschwitz and four of them, all Jews from Poland, came up with a plot to bomb the crematoria – the ovens. They got a hold of some explosives smuggled in by female inmates who were transferred daily to work at a munitions factory sub camp of Auschwitz. Using this material they managed to make bombs which destroyed one of the crematoriums and killed several of the Nazi guards there. Jankiel's name is on a plaque now at the Museum in Auschwitz and if you see the movie *The Grey Zone*, you can see what they did to try and slow down the killings. They were successful in part. But they were captured and they were tortured and killed when the Nazis found out who was responsible.

In 1959 the Radomer Mutual Society – the Radom Mutual Cultural Center of New York – put up a memorial in Long Island at the New Montefiore Cemetery to the Jews from Radom who were murdered. My cousin's book says there were 33,000 of them. My parents and sister and brother-in-law and my little niece are in that number. If you go to the Montefiore Cemetery you will see their names engraved there with the other Jews of Radom who were killed. And that doesn't even include my grandparents who died in Warsaw and all my aunts and uncles and cousins in Warsaw or David's family from Kalish who the Nazis also murdered. Their names are engraved in the Miami Beach Memorial Park.

Marker for my family at the Radomer Society Victims of the Shoah Memorial for Radom victims and survivors in the Montefiore Jewish Cemetery in New York

With everything I've been through, my kids went through a lot with me. The two of them are miracles, miracle kids. In *The Sound of Music* it says, "Nothing comes from nothing, nothing ever could. Somewhere in my life I must have done something good." That's how I feel about my kids and my grandchildren and great-grandchildren too, that somewhere in my life I must have done something good. If I had worries in my life I tried to keep them to myself. I'm such a watchdog by nature. I am always looking over my shoulder to see what might be coming at me or my kids.

No matter how bad things got though we were always a singing family. Irv and his father used to sing at parties too; one of their favorite songs was *If I Were a Rich Man.* Tes' favorite song was always *The Impossible Dream.*

Tes is married to Stuart Schreiber and they live in San Diego. Irv and Mindy live near Boston and I am a grandmother of three and now a great-grandmother of 10. I am proud of my family, of Irv's success and Tes' talent as a singer and a performer and of the kind of people they are, people who are respected. Just like my parents were.

We still own the house in Queens but have been renting it out since none of us lives in New York now, because in September of 2012 Irv and Tes moved me from the house where I lived for almost 50 years to Rhode

68

Island and to Tamarisk. It is the only home for seniors that has kosher food in that part of the country so that's where they moved me.

It was good being nearer to the family. Irv visited me once or twice a week and also some of the grand-children live nearby. The people at Tamarisk were very nice, most of them come from around the Providence area. I got very friendly with the people I sat with at lunch and dinner, especially to another survivor, Fania. She passed away in early 2014 at the age of 100 and I miss her.

David's headstone at the Radomer Society plot on Long Island

But I was going so often back and forth to Tes and Stu in California that the time came for me to live there with them. So, in June 2014 I moved to San Diego to live with my daughter Tes in her own home. A gentleman named Andrew Yachad who had befriended me in New England offered to move to San Diego with me to become my full-time caregiver. Andrew lives with us now in Tes and Stu's home. He takes me to adult care, doctor visits and to temple Friday and Saturday for Shabbat services. The weather and people in San Diego are warm and it's good for me to live with one of my kids, although I do miss seeing Irv and my grandkids and great-grandkids since I now live much further away on the west coast.

Here I still want to be busy. The body says 'no' but I force myself. Still, mostly now what I need is peace. Peace, nothing fancy. I always liked the line from *Porgy and Bess*: "I'm tired of living but scared of dying."

You asked me what I want my family to understand about me. With everyone I've lost, the only thing that's kept me tied to life was taking care of others. As long as I had someone to care for, if it was Frances or my kids or David, that is what makes me strong. This is how I have lived.

No, I was not home when the Nazis came for my parents. My mother took care of that when she forced me to go back to work when I wanted to stay home with them that day. If I had been allowed to stay home either they would not have been taken or I would have gone with them. They were that dear to me. I know my parents would have moved heaven and earth to save me – to them family was everything. They never complained. "Ha Shem will help," they always told us. We may have had less than some others but everything we had looked beautiful to me. My decision not to abort Tes when the doctor told me to do so was easy because I was raised to think that family is everything.

I wanted the same thing for my children that my parents wanted for me: That they should have a good life. I knitted, crocheted and sewed everything for Tes to wear. I wanted Irv to be in a warm place so he went to college in Florida. How can I complain? I survived the war and had two children: two miracles.

And I've realized that, as much as I needed David Kempner after the war – remember he said to me, "As Frances needs you, you need me."? – he really needed me more. But it's been hard. On my left breast where I was so badly beaten, many years later they wanted me to have a biopsy and I said, "No." They wanted to give me an artificial breast and I said "No." After everything I've been through, *dayenu* – enough. An artificial breast would be too much. But when it was time for my husband to have an operation I said, "You are going to the best doctor. Never mind how I pay back the money – $10,000, it was three times as much as my husband was making then. That was the same doctor who told me there's a possibility that, if I could get pregnant, when the milk would flow that it could wash away the growth.

The most powerful force that shaped me? It was to perpetuate my parents. Because of them, no matter what, I would not want to live as a non-Jew, even when the non-Jewish guard wanted to save me and marry me. I could never allow myself to live as a non-Jew, even if it meant being saved. Go off with a non-Jewish guy? Me? Yitzhak Freidenreich's daughter?

I was not religious growing up. My sister Frances was more so. She was a Bais Yaakov girl. But in Auschwitz I was the more religious one. She would say, "How can G-d allow this to happen?" But I didn't want to put the blame on G-d. I told her I had no one else to trust so I had to trust G-d. She asked me how could I be so stupid but I said had to believe in something! The truth is also that taking care of Frances gave me the reason to live. I kept thinking if I could make her better I would have done something that matters.

But I also learned to beware. There is danger and not just from the Nazis. There is still anti-Semitism in the world. People still hate us for our pride in what we are. But I have also learned that if I hear any snide remark, I don't stand for it anymore. I speak up.

The most important lesson I've learned in my life is not to be afraid. I always taught my kids, "If something is hard, don't give up. You'll figure it out." In one of the camps, I was given some raw felt and told I had to make a hat with it. I knew I better make it or else. I was scared because I had no real equipment to work with but I said to myself, "Malka, you have to do it" … And I did.

I'm a bat Kohen – the daughter of a Kohen – so I have to be proud of that too. It was a sense of hope no matter what that I got from my father. He taught me *betachon* – to trust – and to never give up. "Don't ever say you've walked the final road." To the crematorium they were singing this song. A miracle can happen anytime so you can't give up.

My family: My children, grandchildren and now great-grandchildren

What am I proudest of? I went through Hitler and I lived. I know I lived because I had my sister to take care of. But still I lived.

71

A Word From My Children

Irv

When I was a student at the University of Miami, there were very few Jews living in my dorm. Many of my dorm mates belong to R.O.T.C, and offered me the opportunity to go sky-diving with them. I called my mom and dad and they gave me lots of reasons not to do it. Reasons that made sense to them, having lost so much family already. Taking my life in my hands like that was the last thing a survivor would want his beloved child to do. My German-American roommate Art had said to the R.O.T.C guys, "Irv won't do it. He's a Jewish guy from New York." Upon learning of Art's bigoted comments, I falsified my parents' signatures on the permission slip and I went.

When it came my turn, they told me to climb out on the wing. "Jump!" the instructor yelled. And then "Wait!" But by that time I had jumped so I didn't really hear him. It was a very quiet, a very peaceful feeling. At first it's just you falling and then the parachute opens and you know you are going to live. I heard myself singing *Hava Nagila* on the way down. I remember I missed the target and landed softly in the swamp. But I was very proud of myself. I only skydived once but that sense of accomplishment, of pushing past the fear, set the tone for the rest of my life.

I worked myself up from sales rep to the VP of Sales in a Fortune 500 company, having moved my family eight times across the country as I climbed the corporate ladder taking on 13 different positions over a 30-year career.

I've always identified with Joseph in the Torah. Despite all the obstacles in his way Joseph overcame them all to became the number-two man to Pharaoh, the most powerful person in the world at the time. It was a position from which he was able to save his adopted nation and rescue his family. His father Yaakov once he was reunited with his powerful son after 22 years, wondered about Joseph's commitment to his monotheistic upbringing. "But is he still a Jew?" The answer was: Yes, he was still a proud Jew and a capable secular leader. And so am I.

On the March of the Living I witnessed the towns my parents came from. Walking through their neighborhoods, the ghettos and the death camps deepened my understanding of what our families went through and what we the Jewish people must try to rebuild. It also helped me appreciate my parents' drive to survive and the strength of the human spirit to overcome tragedy and go on.

My parents' lives, two souls that were saved by the US Army in April 1 and May 5, 1945, resulted in the growth and perpetuation of a new Jewish world here in America. A world that now includes me and my wife Mindy, my sister Tes and her husband Stu, three proud and accomplished Jewish grandchildren, my kids Batyah, Benjay and Jeremy who also found three wonderful, intelligent and humorous life partners, Benji, Marissa and Kim. All of whom are productive citizens with meaningful careers and community affiliations. And of course my kids have produced 10 beautiful great-grandchildren. Such *nachus*.

Hitler won two victories: ridding Europe of its Jews and destroying

Irv and me

our *rachmonis* (compassion) for each other in that generation. But the survivors were survivors because they made tough choices. They say that in every generation there are 32 *tzaddikim* alive to keep the world going. Today we can be victims or we can be proud Jews, persecuted or respected by the world. It's our choice. I choose to be respected.

Her greatest triumph is that, having lived through the horrors she experienced, my mom has been able to live to see children, grandchildren and great-grandchildren, new families who were created and able to thrive as proud Jews only because she survived.

Tes

My mother is the most challenging, compelling, steadfast human being I have ever known. The strength – and stubbornness – of her character have intimidated, frustrated, and ultimately tempered my own to a level of both compassion and resilience beyond anything I could have predicted possible!

They say what doesn't kill you makes you stronger. What my mother has survived and endured has cultivated such an indomitable spirit, it would not surprise anyone we know if she outlived us all!

Where I am ready to quit, she is ready to push on. Where my heart has seemed too wounded to reopen, she forgives and embraces and loves again. And again. And again. And again.

There is a part of me that is so "over" this difficult and inhumane world, so over the challenges of my family tragedy and the subsequent relentless karma in my role as daughter of Holocaust Survivors, that I can sometimes long for oblivion. That my mother perseveres - and generally still wants to be here – forces me to keep climbing too. She is remarkable.

Tes wearing one of the thousands of hats I made over the years

Recently I attended a women's event where we were asked what one quality of our mother's we most admired and would wish to embody, or emulate. Unhesitatingly, I said, "dignity." My mother's dignity has made an indelible impression on my soul ... and I will carry this awareness with me for all my days.

My friends recognize my mother as a heroine, a saint ... an international treasure. I witness in awe and pride. The difficult parts of being my mother's daughter are so intense ... bordering on unconscious psycho-emotional abuse, unreasonable expectations and near non-existent boundaries. Yet the beauty of her well-meaning *neshama* keeps me her loyal devotee for as long as I am graced with the blessing of her existence.

For years, I have attempted to wean myself in preparation of this ultimate loss. It is no use. When she is gone, despite some imagined relief at the end of her torment, I am certain I will miss her deeply. Knowing I have done everything in my power to bring some happiness to her own wounded little girl ... yet never fully succeeding. So many songs I have written to cheer and immortalize her!

Life is miraculous and divine. Yet it is not fair. If reincarnation is real, I pray that we meet again – under sweeter circumstances – and can laugh together at last in the awakening from this very strange dream.

With all the love in my heart …

Tes

Writer's Postscript

Since the moment we met, just after Pesach of 2013, I interviewed Marlena some 14 times, for four hours-plus each sitting. There were days when she cried and there were days when we cried together. And there were also times when we laughed. I learned early on that Marlena didn't like me sitting at the kitchen table pecking away at my laptop, but repeatedly patted the couch, entreating me to sit by her. After the first two visits, I left my laptop at home and took notes longhand, looking up often to observe her expressions and reassure her with my eyes that I understood. By summer I knew the stories of her life as well as her family, stories I learned not to interrupt since they were like a song where I knew the lyrics and the tune but needed to hear them again and again to fully absorb what this amazing woman had experienced and the courage that had seen her through it all. So I could understand what it meant to live her life well enough to do it justice in words. At each interview's end Marlena was exhausted and emotionally drained but she never failed to ask me about my children and grandchildren and how my plans to move to Israel were coming along.

I feel truly blessed that Marlena's family invited me to spend the better part of the last year listening to and bearing witness to her story, a story the numbers on her forearm, as faded and wrinkled as they are, continue to bear another kind of witness to.

I have written other books, and have won awards for my writing. But I have never thanked my Creator for any assignment like I thanked Him for this one ... and for the tremendous honor of earning even a small sliver of this survivor's trust. One misunderstanding in fact proved to be especially rewarding. "I didn't know you were writing a book!" she scolded me as we were finishing up that summer. "I thought you were just a friend who wanted to hear my stories." And so it came to be. I was by then a friend who wanted to hear her stories. And yes, to record them in the book you now hold in your hands.

Although my deepest gratitude is to Marlena for taking me into her thoughts and feelings, the pain and even the wonder of those times, I also wish to thank the Kempner family for entrusting their mother and her story to me at this vulnerable time in her life. For giving me full access to her and to the photos and links and documents that helped her life come alive for me. Empowering me to tell this story of love and redemption, a story as sacred as it is painful.

May the memories set down here prove a worthy monument to the lost world Marlena has been given the years, the *koach* – and the courage – to take us back to. May these words strengthen and empower our people. And remind us and future generations that we truly stand both on the shoulders of giants and under the wings of the Almighty.

Deborah Fineblum
Maale Adumim, Israel
April 23, 2015
4 Iyar, 5775

<hr />

For more information about Marlene and her story, contact IrvKempner@gmail.com

40416868R00055